HUMAN RELATIONS IN ACTION

Problems and Cases in
Dealing with People

HUMAN RELATIONS IN ACTION

Problems and Cases in Dealing with People

BY

Calvin C. Thomason

*Formerly, Head of Department
of the Social Sciences
Rochester Institute of Technology*

AND

Frank A. Clement

*Chairman of the General Education Division
Rochester Institute of Technology*

SECOND EDITION

GREENWOOD PRESS, PUBLISHERS
WESTPORT, CONNECTICUT

Introduction

THIS BOOK is the result of more than twenty-five years of active effort to provide a guide for discussion groups that seek better understanding of human capabilities, habits, and attitudes. The resulting selection of subject matter for its functional value is one of the distinctive features of the book. It combines some of the more immediately applicable values of the traditional, introductory course in psychology with equally applicable principles that are found in nontechnical writings directed to the layman who is interested in bettering his human relationships.

A second distinctive feature is the "multiple-case" method of arrangement and presentation of material. The second half of each unit of study comprises questions and brief cases that embody the principles involved in each unit. The discussion of these questions and cases acts as a "detonator" or "springboard" for the introduction of additional cases from the experiences of the group members.

The term *case* refers to brief, pointed incidents that focus attention on particular principles, facts, or phases of human reaction; also to terse quotations of types of thinking that are valuable for group analysis.

The first advantage of this method is that individuals of widely differing background profit by the interchange of case applications, and each may take from the discussion the ideas he is best able to assimilate and apply.

Again, the multiple-case method avoids set rules or slogans. It requires the reader to search for facts, to apply principles, and to think out solutions logically.

A third advantage is that the group itself becomes a human relations laboratory. Members must listen attentively, analyze carefully, and respect the opinions of others. This leads to growth in self-control, straight thinking, and human understanding.

Two purposes stand behind this revision of the book:

1. To re-arrange the units and some of the material in the units to better meet the needs of the users of the first edition.

2. To provide for the inclusion of new or revised concepts needed by any book that is closely dependent upon so new and growing a science as psychology.

In making this adaptation to fit current needs, every effort has been made not to lose the vigor of Mr. Thomason's original, pioneering approach to the important field of human relations. Mr. Thomason had accumulated some notes for a revision, and also had frequently discussed his ideas with this writer, so it can be said that the original author has a hand in the revision. Other suggestions have come from the group leaders in Management in the Evening Division, and from the Psychology Committee, of the Rochester Institute of Technology. Special thanks are due Walter E. Rauch, Chairman of the Department of General Education at Westchester Community College for the helpful suggestions that resulted from his understanding reading of the manuscript.

Frank A. Clement

Contents

UNIT I

Human Nature

Objectives

1. *To become aware of basic human drives and desires.*
2. *To recognize how these basic drives and desires are modified by habit or learning.*
3. *To increase ability to work with, instead of against, human nature.*
4. *To establish the habit of treating every person as an individual.*
5. *To recognize the importance of emotions in all human relations.*

INTRODUCTION

"John doesn't seem to be acting natural these days."

Ordinarily this statement would sound like a casual enough observation, but as an introduction to this book it should be given more than passing consideration. What do we mean by "natural"? Do we mean natural for John or natural for anybody? How different is John's nature from the nature of other people? Is there a nature common to all human beings? Is it *natural* to be a grouch—or a good mixer? Were the grouches or the good mixers born that way, or did they get that way because of experiences they have had? Were they affected both by their inherited characteristics and their experiences in life? A question, then, to keep in mind is: "What are *natural* actions?"

We sometimes hear people speak of an idea as "going against human nature." We seldom stop to ask just what they mean by "human nature"; instead, it is assumed that everyone knows what it is. However, if we are going to make a study of dealing with people, it is appropriate to ask what we do mean by a basic term like this, and, in trying to organize an answer, we shall already find ourselves beginning to understand both our fellowbeings and ourselves a little better.

Let's look for a moment at the sort of study that we are undertaking. Some indication of the road to be traveled during this course may be obtained by examining three summary ideas. The first defines the broad field of *psychology*, in which the study of human relations lies:

"Psychology is a science which seeks to find out how and why individuals and groups act as they do, the respects in which they are similar and in which they are different, and the way in which they are influenced by their environment. It seeks light on the original nature of people, on their acquired traits and on the way in which they acquire them, on the resulting modifications of human nature, on the relation of human nature and human nurture." [1]

The second idea suggests particular applications of the principles to be presented in this book:

"Underneath all *leadership* lies the bedrock nature of man. We cannot understand the factors of *leadership* without understanding adult human behavior. Whether we agree with those who stress hereditary influences or those who stress environment, we must understand and evaluate the individual's reactions to working and machine conditions, to monotony, to standards of performance, to orders, to instructions and supervision by others, and to rewards." [2]

Metcalf speaks here of *leadership;* but students of human relations will do well to use also the companion term *followership* in the same context, since we live in a co-operative society and, if there are leaders, there must be followers. In fact, one could go one step further and also substitute the term *individual maturity* in the last quotation, for our study has the dual objective of learning how to deal effectively with *one's self* as well as with other people.

[1] Tead, Ordway, *Human Nature and Management.*
[2] Metcalf, Henry C., *American Management Association Reports.* New York: McGraw-Hill Book Co., Inc.

The third summary idea involves the theme of this first unit of the book:

"To deal with a man without account of his pride, inertia, self-respect, fears, stupidities, loyalty, and personality is to deal with a slot machine, not a man." [3]

The gradual understanding of this last idea is what has lain behind the development in recent times of personnel programs in industry and business. This is why so many modern executives, teachers, or parents *suggest* or *inspire* rather than command. Throughout time the growth and spread of religious doctrines, philosophies, and political ideologies have developed from someone's understanding of the needs and concerns of the individual. Today ordinary people in great numbers are gaining knowledge of what in past centuries seemed to be the particular possession of a few outstanding leaders —that to work with human nature pays dividends, whereas to work against it invites disaster.

THE HEREDITARY POINT OF VIEW

From the beginning of life in the fertilized germ cell, each individual is different in some way from every other. As Elizabeth Gregg MacGibbon says, "Part of the great mystery of all nature is that there are no duplicates. In his factories man turns out hundreds, thousands, or even millions of duplicates. But not so in the great universe." [4] No two leaves, no two snowflakes, no two people (not even identical twins) are just alike. This principle of individuality is known as *variation*.

However, accepting these variations, there are also certain fundamental characteristics of human beings that are possessed by practically all people. It would help set the stage for a study of human nature if we presented briefly some of these common characteristics.

1. It is generally agreed that human beings inherit certain basic individual physical and mental equipment. This includes

[3] Dennison, H. S., *American Management Association Reports.*
[4] *Fitting Yourself for Business.* New York: McGraw-Hill Book Co., Inc., 1947.

sense organs, muscles, glands, and the brain and nerve equipment upon which the ability or capacity to learn depends. In other words, we are born with a body that functions and with a mind which is a physiological part of that body and largely directs its activity. This seems almost too obvious to mention, but it needs to be considered seriously for the reason that so much of human behavior results from the very nature of the body as a living organism.

2. Any living organism—and most certainly the human body, which is the most complex living organism—depends upon certain materials and conditions for the very maintenance of life. These include food, moisture, repair through rest, reproduction, and tolerable temperature. Therefore we inherit, along with our bodies, certain basic urges or drives such as hunger, thirst, the compulsion to sleep, the sex drive, and the impulse to protect ourselves from the elements. A little thinking will show that if a body were not accompanied by these basic drives it might very well "forget" to go on living.

3. We seem also to inherit a small number of reflexes—activities or reaction patterns that are not directed by the conscious mind—such as the knee-jerk reflex, or the closing of the eyelids if a bright light is flashed. Reflexes are often called *instincts* as they become more involved, and they are observable in greater number and importance in studying the activities of lower forms of life. A mud wasp, for instance, seems much more controlled by instinct than by reasoning, whereas the behavior of man, as the most reasoning of animals, seems to be the least controlled by instincts or reflexes.

4. There is yet another drive possessed by all organisms that arises from their active striving to *seek the satisfying* and *avoid the unsatisfying*. That is the drive for *security*. In mankind this gives rise to a series of common characteristics that need special attention in this unit on Human Nature. The first of these is *curiosity*, without which we could hardly find out what to seek or what to avoid in our struggle for security. Another is the *desire for recognition*, which, when satisfied, furnishes a

sort of spiritual security and at best may even lead to some material security. A third common characteristic is *rivalry* or *competitiveness*, which enables man to achieve certain of the satisfactions of life that seem not to exist in sufficient quantity for all people to enjoy as they would like. A fourth is *gregariousness*, or the wanting to herd together for the security to be gained from being with other people. A fifth is *creativeness*, or the drive to do, to make, to achieve, or in some way to modify our environment for our greater satisfaction. All of these—curiosity, desire for recognition, rivalry, gregariousness, and creativeness—vary from individual to individual only in degree. They are worth our particular attention because once we realize that they are not only a vital part of our own make-up, but also vital in the make-up of every individual we meet, we have already begun to build an understanding of people that will help us in all our associations with them.

So much for the primary drives of mankind, which we may consider *nonlearned* inasmuch as they seem to be a part of our equipment at birth.

The problem of making fine distinctions between the nonlearned and the learned in human behavior is as difficult as it is interesting, but it must be left for the specialists in that area of science. *Learning* begins after conception and continues throughout life. Therefore, the behavior and disposition of a human individual soon become complex combinations of not only his basic drives but also his acquired habits and desires. It is now a well-established principle that men's lives are molded by the interaction of heredity and environment. The following are but two of many statements of this point of view:

1. "We may now dismiss the old debate as to whether environment is more important than heredity. Scientists now know that both have tremendous significance. . . . Environment is like the photographer's developing chemical: It creates nothing, but it can bring out what is on the film." [5]

2. Changes in any object—a piece of steel, a piece of ice,

[5] Bruce Bliven, *Reader's Digest.*

a machine, an organism—depend upon the material of which it is composed, and upon the conditions in which it exists. . . . Organisms are like other objects in this respect; what they do or become depends both on their components and the conditions surrounding them. The dependence on the original make-up we call heredity. But no single thing that the organism does depends alone on heredity or alone on environment; always, both must be taken into account.[6]

To illustrate the foregoing general discussion in terms of practical applications, we can list a hereditary drive and place opposite it one of its many modified developments in life:

HEREDITARY[7] (Native, or inborn)	ENVIRONMENTAL (Learned, or developed)
To be hungry.	To eat broiled steak with a knife and fork.
To make vocal sounds.	To speak English.
To desire the company of people.	To invite friends in for a game of bridge.
To be curious.	To conduct research in nuclear fission.
To compete.	To play basketball.
To seek a comfortable temperature.	To build a heating plant.

To pursue this subject further would be to go beyond the scope of this course. The important matter here is not the relative importance of heredity or environment, nor is it the precise dividing line between the two. Rather, the important point is to observe *what are* the basic drives of human nature as they exist in people of various positions and varying ages, and to remember that each person is going to modify them in accordance with his environment.

[6] Jennings, H. S., *Prometheus: or Biology and the Advancement of Man.* New York: E. P. Dutton & Co.

[7] These are called hereditary in this unit for purposes of simplification. Science has not yet found adequate means for determining what is strictly hereditary.

HABIT (OR LEARNING)

The term *habit*, in its broadest sense, includes all reactions that are *learned*. That we act at all may be due to native or "instinctive" drives; the *way* we act is determined by the learning we do—in other words, by the habits we form. Definitely then, the learner, on the one hand, and the supervisor of learners, on the other hand, are both primarily interested in the development of useful habits, that is, useful *skills* and *attitudes*.

It is impossible to teach an idiot to read, to make a musical artist of someone who is tone deaf, or to produce a good typist from someone lacking co-ordination. Trying to do so gives us nothing but "square pegs in round holes." But where two persons may have nearly equal mental and physical endowment, whether one becomes a grocery clerk and the other an engineer will largely depend on the habits they form, that is, the learning they do, or their *education*, whether it be undertaken in or out of schools. Education, or the development of skills and attitudes, is probably the determining factor in whether a person becomes an artist or a scientist, a radical or a conservative, a crook or a clergyman. In general, supervisors, trainers for special skills, or classroom teachers may assume that the groups they are given to work with are relatively alike in the necessary endowments for learning the work. This assumption is possible thanks to a whole series of accidental factors, as well as to discriminating employment offices, testing programs, and merit-rating systems. The job of the supervisor, trainer, or teacher, then, is to train the individuals in the habits they need to perform.

Habit formation is not merely negative. It is true that one has formed habits if he is forever swearing, or a victim of cigarettes, or is never on time. But habit also consists of more than these negative reactions. If one can look at another person and greet him by name, he has formed a habit. If one can now enjoy oysters when he once could not, he has formed a habit. If one can stay at an evening of constructive work when his friends are trying to lure him to a party or a theater, he is profiting by trained work habits. If one has learned how to be calm and courteous rather than sulky and antagonistic in the face of what looks like unjust criticism, he has been developing constructive emotional habits. And so on—a list could comprise thousands of habits ranging from walking, eating, and speaking to playing a concert or figuring the distance of a star. Every person, whether he be a supervisor or an operative, a teacher or a student, an officer or a private, a club leader or a rank-and-file club member, must utilize a countless number of habits in making himself effective in his material, economic, and human environment. Perhaps it could be inferred from this that the greatest of all habits would be *the habit of forming new habits.*

Human habits may be grouped in three broad divisions:

1. *Motor, or muscular habits.* These include the familiar work skills, athletics, and other activities in which the primary measure is the handling of tools or other equipment with speed and accuracy. Of course a mental factor, clear understanding, and emotional factors, such as confidence and interest, also function here, but the identifying characteristic of these habits is that they mainly involve motor, or muscular, ability.

2. *Mental habits.* As will be pointed out later, the brain is vitally involved as the directive center of almost all bodily reactions. However, certain habits, like the learning of names, multiplication tables, price lists, and literary quotations, or the reasoning processes, such as logical analysis and the building of associational patterns, are habits that lie much more in the area of mentality than in muscles or emotions, and may be classed as mental habits.

3. *Emotional habits.* These are the *attitudes,* such as confidence, interest, liking or disliking, hate, fear, prejudice, love, etc. True, these attitudes exist in the mind and are therefore somewhat mental, yet they have something in addition to sheer

mentality. This book will discuss emotions in more detail in a later unit. Perhaps, for the present, one might distinguish between emotional habits and mental habits by first asking himself what his attitude, or habit of thinking, may be in connection with his landlord, his mother-in-law, or his boss, and then asking himself how much emotion is involved in the mental habit, $3 \times 3 = 9$.

Influences reaching back into early childhood often give rise to emotional habits that may help or hinder the adult. A child unjustly punished or scared may carry attitudes of fear, suspicion, or self-doubt into all of his adult activities and may take these attitudes for granted simply because he does not remember their origins. Wherever groups are at work, study, or play, a vicious or idle rumor, an impatient or indistinct order, or an innovation for which others are not prepared may set up strong detrimental attitudes that take time, skill, and poise to correct.

It is interesting to reflect that, in the history of human learning, the kinds of knowledge that most directly affect man himself as an individual have usually been the last to be studied or discovered. The ancients knew a great deal about astronomy, but it has taken modern times to give much scientific study to agriculture. The philosophy of Aristotle was given to the world 2000 years before steam or electric power was used. Similarly, only in recent years has serious study been given to human nature. It is not difficult to find supervisors who are expert in the teaching of motor and mental skills, but only a few, seemingly, are conscious of the scope and importance of *emotional habit formation*.

ATTITUDES AND EMPLOYMENT

The attitudes of an employee are of vital importance both to himself and to his employer. He produces for the employer, and the employer furnishes the place to work, the materials to work on, the wage, and the opportunities for advancement. With each new condition, or process, or personal contact, the employee stands at a sort of emotional fork in the road. Shall he take the positive or the negative—the road to adjustment or to maladjustment—the road of progress or of slipping backward?

An employee gets his first impressions of a supervisor and of his employer during his first days on the job. First impressions often may be lasting ones, but whether lasting or not, they are helping to form a series of attitudes. The temper, the imagination, or the sensitivity of an individual can be so mishandled that his attitudes become antagonistic and therefore less productive, or, on the other hand, those same characteristics can be well handled and developed into driving forces that lead to rapid progress in efficiency and personal value. It is quite true that an employee has his own responsibilities for his future. However, the supervisor is the key man and may often be the most important single influence in the employee's life. He has the vital contacts with the most necessary part of the employee's existence—the job—upon which the employee's security and progress depend.

We anticipate trouble in machines and motors because we know the danger signals. The maintenance man avoids breakdowns by timely oiling, greasing, or minor repairs. In much the same way, a doctor anticipates heart conditions and other ailments by interpreting symptoms. Then he prescribes rest, diet, or other preventive remedy for his patient. The alert supervisor, by knowing background and basic human nature, can see when a bad attitude is developing in his working force. If he senses such a situation in time, he may apply a preventive remedy while the trouble is yet only minor. If he overlooks the impending difficulty until it becomes a major problem, the result may be the loss of a good employee, an increase in departmental cost, the creation of an embarrassing situation for himself, or some other experience that he will have to live down.

So, when anyone who has to deal with other people makes

the mental note, "John (or Mary) doesn't seem to be acting natural these days," an understanding of the motivating forces behind human behavior may enable him to prevent many problems from arising. For example, if he knows that John is worried about a sick child or a wife who is spending too much of his wages on clothes, or that Mary has an invalid mother and does all of the housework after she gets home, he may, in his treatment of them on the job, avoid unsatisfactory handling that would cause tempers to flare. An ounce of prevention is always worth its pound of cure.

Problem I

Why is it difficult to distinguish between native urges and learned traits? In our everyday dealings with people, is it necessary to draw such distinctions sharply?

CASE 1

When the mother wasp gathers a store of food suitable for young larvae, lays an egg beside the food, and covers the whole with a wall of mud, she has had no opportunity to learn from older wasps. When last year's crop of nests was being made she was only an unhatched egg.

Newly hatched birds kept in cages out of sight of adult birds fly readily enough as soon as their wings are sufficiently strong.

What does a human infant know how to do?

Is it hungry?

Does it know how to eat?

CASE 2

Particular ways of satisfying native urges or reaction patterns may become considerably altered *even among animals*. Certain cliff swallows have been known to desert the cliffs and begin building their nests under the eaves of houses as a territory becomes settled.

It is said that European beavers no longer build huts and dams, but now dig burrows.

Are there *reasons* for these altered reaction patterns?

CASE 3

Are some habits formed unconsciously?

Is a person taught to suck his thumb, to bite his nails, to fidget with his earlobe or mouth?

Could a large amount of learning throughout life go on more or less unconsciously?

Problem II

What are some of the drives that people tend to have in common?

CASE 1

During one summer, W, a twelve-year-old boy, cut up cedar fence rails, split miniature boards, and constructed a little city on a sandy knoll near a brook; he built a bridge across the stream and put a small water wheel in a waterfall nearby. Today, W is general foreman of a department that can always be counted on to be in order and to set production records. He is never content with the status of things, but is constantly improving machines, processes, and organization in his department.

CASE 2

As a youngster, X was constantly investigating things. He once was caught in a trap while trying to find out how it worked. At school he took up each subject expecting to discover something new. Today, studies of a broader nature are his most enjoyable recreation—studies that throw light upon the meaning and purpose of his work in the factory and of his environment outside the factory.

CASE 3

In school, Y studied hardest and liked best those subjects in which he received most recognition from his teachers. If an older brother would let him drive the tractor and would notice the favorable things he did, or if a neighbor would praise his work, he was quick to run errands and was reliable in all assignments for such people. As an executive now, Y is the real leader of his department because he is big enough to *give credit where it is due* and to correct errors *without display of emotion*.

CASE 4

In the case of Z, a biography might be written around his long list of sham battles with pine-cone artillery, neighborhood bouts with boxing gloves, or contests in running, jumping, or other youthful accomplishment. Well along in middle life, he now finds "whipping a new job" as thrilling as he once found beating the town bully. His organization knows to whom to look in a difficulty or when a rush order comes in.

Problem III

Will it help an individual in his dealings with people to recognize and make allowances for the drives in human nature?

CASE 1

It is sometimes helpful to think of the *ego* as a sort of imaginary bladder or balloon that we like to keep properly inflated. As the physical self feels content with a nicely filled stomach, so does the emotional self feel content with a nicely rounded "ego-balloon." Consequently we devour any compliment we can get and even dream up self-complimentary ideas to feed our ego. People seem to be more eagerly concerned about feeding their "ego-balloons" than their physical selves, and a great deal of human behavior can be understood in terms of this "ego-hunger."

How much co-operation do you feel like giving the person who treats you more or less as though you were a bungling moron "and he'll try to put up with you since he somehow got stuck with you"?

How much co-operation do you give the person who is human enough to see that you have intelligence, fairmindedness, ambition, and a warm, engaging personality?

Do you think other people would feel the same toward you if you acted in either one of these ways?

Is co-operation important?

CASE 2

A foreman overheard one workman making fun of another and sensed that the second one was hurt. He called the first man into his office, and said: "John, I have always had a good deal of respect for you. I have always felt that you were very considerate. You did not realize how you made that man feel. You know, it is not everyone who can take a good jibe and let it roll off easily. Walter happens to be a sensitive fellow. I just wanted to call this to your attention." [8]

What difference does it make to the foreman whether John "needles" Walter?

Did the foreman handle John smoothly?

Invent other ways that this situation might have been handled, with different results.

CASE 3

A certain football coach is reputed to have an unhappy faculty for "rubbing the boys the wrong way." A few days before the — game last fall, a young man slammed a football to the turf in disgust and turned in his uniform because the coach was humiliating him before his teammates.

In another college there was the best supply of football material in the district, but the team was barely able to win half its games. Players frequently stumbled through practice plays blindly, not knowing what they were supposed to do, because they knew that to ask questions of the coach would bring down torrents of abuse.

Is humiliation more deflating to the ego in the presence of other people than when alone?

Which is abuse more apt to achieve, wholehearted co-operation or grudging participation?

The methods used by successful coaches seem to be based on:
1. Clear and decisive instructions.
2. Approval of good plays.
3. Analysis and discussion of errors.

Discuss how these three ideas fit with the human characteristics mentioned under the discussion of *security* on pages 4 and 5 of the preview of this unit.

CASE 4

It is related that an American cigarette manufacturer operating in a primitive foreign district was losing production on account of serious absenteeism. The wants of his girl workers were so simple that they chose to work a day or two each week and take the rest of the time off. He picked out the prettiest girl in the factory, presented her with a pair of nylons, and explained that each of the

[8] Shellow, S. M., *Personnel Series, No. 24.* New York: American Management Association.

others would get a similar gift if her attendance were regular. He repeated this sort of approach, now and then, by offering portable record players and other luxuries to the point where he had raised the living standards of the community. Steady work became essential to anyone who wished to maintain this new standard.

What did the manufacturer want? Did he get it?

What basic drive was he appealing to?

CASE 5

"Once when I was with Mr. Carnegie," wrote Charles M. Schwab,[9] "I had a mill manager who was finely educated, thoroughly capable, and master of every detail of the business. But he seemed unable to inspire his men to do their best.

"'How is it that a man as able as you,' I asked him one day, 'cannot make this mill turn out what it should?'

"'I don't know,' he replied. 'I have coaxed the men; I have pushed them; I have sworn at them. I have done everything in my power. Yet they will not produce.'

"It was near the end of the day; in a few minutes the night shift would come on duty. I turned to one of the workmen who was standing beside one of the red-mouthed furnaces and asked him for a piece of chalk.

"'How many heats has your shift made today?' I queried.

"'Six,' he replied.

"I chalked a big '6' on the floor, and passed along without another word. When the night shift came in they saw the '6' and asked about it.

"'The big boss was in here today,' said the day men. 'He asked us how many heats we turned out, and we told him six. He chalked it down.'

"The next morning as I passed through the same mill I saw that the '6' had been rubbed out and a big '7' written instead. The night shift had announced itself. That night I went back. The '7' had been erased and a '10' swaggered in its place."

What basic drive was Mr. Schwab appealing to when he wrote a "6" on the floor?

What basic drive helped accomplish the increase in production?

---

[9] Schwab, Charles M., *Succeeding With What You Have*. New York: Century Co., 1917.

Problem IV

Is the development of emotional skills as well understood and utilized as is the development of motor and mental skills?

CASE 1

As soon as the infant is old enough to be attracted by bright objects, a toy is dangled above its head. Whereupon it looks, gurgles, kicks, squirms, and frets. When its random arm movements bring its hands in the direction of the toy, the holder of the toy meets the right movement halfway and the child grasps the toy. It soon learns that reaching for the toy brings surest satisfaction, and it rapidly drops all the unnecessary movements and activities. The reaching reaction has been learned—has become a fixed habit.

Has emotion had anything to do with the learning of this motor skill?

CASE 2

In a certain establishment, the practice fire alarm bell rings at definitely fixed times known to the working force. The men are away from their machines and ready to march out when the gong sounds.

It is reported that certain football coaches allow approximately four seconds for a drop kick in practice, but when in action the kicker has, on the average, about two seconds.

Are habits being formed in these training situations?

What is liable to be added when the real situation occurs?

How might the training be done so as to prepare for the emergency?

CASE 3

X now realizes that his greatest handicap has been a lack of confidence in his judgments. Why this weakness? Well, for one thing, when he was a youngster the chief source of fun among his older brothers and his father were his childish ideas and expressions. Throughout his life he has been good at jobs in which his superiors expressed confidence in him, but uncertain and inefficient when there was no such expression of confidence.

Who is responsible for X's present inefficiency?

If X worked for you, could you improve his efficiency?

CASE 4

"The loyalty which the employees had for the Blank Public Service Company was built up over a period of years to a point where each employee felt certain that he was working for, and really was a part of, the fairest and finest corporation in the world. . . . 'Things are different now,' writes Baxter, 'things' meaning employees' loyalty and attitude toward the Blank Public Service Company. . . . As the depression dragged along, labor turnover was reduced to practically zero. . . . The majority of those in supervisory capacities therefore welcomed what appeared to be the end of their labor problems. They saw their way open to be 'real bosses,' to handle their employees as they saw fit, with no fear of a worker quitting. And so the attitude toward the worker became, in the words of the average supervisor, *you ought to be glad you've got a job.* . . . Before the onslaught of the attitude typified by this statement, employee loyalty was annihilated. In a few months the supervisory force threw away a valuable asset accumulated only through long years of patient recognition." [10]

Why does Viteles refer to the former attitude of the employees as a "valuable asset"?

Is this matter of emotional habit formation worth anything in dollars and cents?

CASE 5

A young supervisor was interested in learning all about the product his department was turning out. He stopped frequently beside a certain machine and examined the trays of pieces because he knew that the operator of this machine was one of the best. One day when he did this, the woman operator sprang to her feet and angrily screamed, "I'm quitting right now if you feel you have to watch me all the time!"

What could the supervisor have done in order that this situation need not have arisen?

Should only supervisors understand ego and emotions, or could the operator have done anything to avoid this occurrence?

CASE 6

Toward the close of the month, a division head of a large office made the last-minute discovery that a certain amount of overtime

[10] Viteles, M. S., *The Science of Work*. New York: W. W. Norton Co.

would be necessary in order to clear up an accumulation of work. When he asked one of his best and most co-operative employees to help him out, she refused, and later in the day handed in her resignation. Inquiry revealed that some time ago this woman had turned in a suggestion that would have taken care of this very accumulation of work. Her suggestion had not been acted upon nor even acknowledged by the division head.

What was been done to this employee's ego?

What kind of attitude is she apt to develop?

Case 7

In a study recently made among motormen in a street-railway system, one-third of all accidents were attributed to attitudes—impulsiveness, nervousness, worry, and depression.

In 400 cases studied in one industrial organization, over 50 per cent of the accidents occurred when the employees stated that they were "feeling low."

Can an observant supervisor, teacher, or parent profit by learning to detect emotional changes in others?

Can activities of work assignments sometimes be changed to suit such a situation?

If the activities cannot be changed, is there anything to be gained by creating as agreeable an atmosphere as possible?

UNIT II

The Nervous System and Habit

Objectives

1. *To recognize the nervous system as a functional basis for all human behavior.*
2. *To understand that there is a physical basis of habit formation.*
3. *To improve observation.*
4. *To appreciate more fully the educational values of work.*

INTRODUCTION

In the previous unit attention was drawn to two basic ideas: first, that a human being is born with a complex of urges and drives; second, that he immediately sets about a lifelong program of learning, or habit-forming, by means of which he conducts or modifies his behavior. The drives are what urge him to act; then he learns how to act. Since learning is so important a phase of human life, it is worthwhile to give brief attention to the equipment, or physiological mechanisms, by means of which man learns.

The aim of this unit is not to present a study of the nervous system as such, but to develop a little understanding of the fascinating but highly involved way in which the nervous system serves man as a tool for learning. A technical study of the nervous system may be very difficult; even the greatest specialists are not yet sure of all the answers. However, the layman can learn some things that may help him with the practical problems of living, just as he can learn enough to drive his car reasonably without knowing all the intricacies of physics involved in its creation or operation. Some basic vocabulary will be necessary and useful here, but the technical terminology of the neurologist will be kept at a minimum. This unit will consider only those parts of the nervous system that the anatomist knows as the *central* and *peripheral* systems. A third system will be observed in a later unit.

Co-ordination

Sketchily, then, the nervous system consists of complicated series of filaments that conduct messages all over the body, much as wires carry electric charges wherever they reach. These filaments of nerve tissue are called *neurons,* and the messages that travel through them are called *impulses.* The brain, or, more properly, that part of the brain called the *cerebral cortex,* is where consciousness, awareness, and thought occur. However, the brain is all snugly concealed in the skull where it cannot without help know anything beyond itself. There must be a system of "news gatherers" sending impulses to the brain that it translates into various kinds of impressions before it, in turn, sends impulses back to various parts of the body in order to control behavior. The "news gatherers" are called *sense receptors,* and they are located near the surface or deeply within the body, according to the sort of *stimuli* that they are supposed to report. A *stimulus* is anything that occurs inside or outside of the body concerning which a sense receptor is able to communicate impulses to the brain, for example, a stomach-ache, the screech of a siren, or the aroma of coffee.

Receptors. The sense receptors may be classified loosely under eight major headings. The first five are the traditional "five senses"—sight, hearing, smell, taste, and the tactile senses. The term "tactile senses" replaces "touch" inasmuch as there are at least specialized temperature, pain, and pressure receptors, and possibly others to be discovered. However, a body would be ill equipped indeed if it were to be limited to the familiar five senses. A sixth all-important kind of sense is the *kinesthetic,* or motion-reporting, sense whose receptors are located throughout the muscles and report to the brain how much a muscle is contracted or relaxed. All of our controlled body movements depend upon this sense. A seventh sense, and one closely coordinated with the kinesthetic, is *equilibrium,* or the sense of balance, the receptors of which are located in the labyrinths of the ears. The need for, and continual use of, this sense becomes obvious with the observation of the senseless lack of control of a person who is dizzy. The eighth classification may be termed *organic,* and be permitted to cover all the receptors that are located in or near organs within the body and report to the brain that the individual is hungry, or satisfied, or must yawn, or needs to seek the relief of elimination, etc.

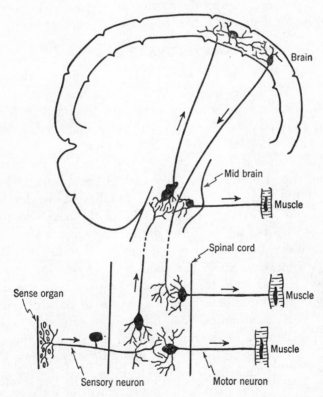

Fig. 1. Connection of First, Second, and Third Levels of the Nervous System. Adapted from Gates, *Elementary Psychology,* by permission of the Macmillan Company.

Neurons. Our brief glance at the nervous system will require that we observe three sorts of neurons. (a) *Sensory neurons* include the sense receptors and extend all the way from where the sense receptor is located to the spinal cord. Sensory neurons convey impulses from the receptors IN to the spinal cord. (b) *Connecting neurons* are located in the spinal cord and brain, and these convey impulses to the brain, throughout the various parts of the brain, and down the spinal cord. (c) *Motor neurons* extend from the spinal cord all the way to some *reactor* and convey impulses from the spinal cord OUT to the reactors. Impulses travel, on the average, at a speed of about 400 feet-per-second, and they jump from sensory, to connecting, to motor neurons in their route from receptors to reactors.

MUSCLES AND GLANDS

Reactors. A reactor is some muscle or gland. There are two types of muscles and of glands. Interestingly enough, the more important muscles and glands, from the point of view of human emotional behavior, are the more difficult to observe directly and, therefore, they are less well known.

Striped muscles. The most easily observable of the reactors are the striped muscles that take care of the mechanical handling of the body. They consist of bundles of slender fibers and vary in size from the big muscles of the back and thighs to the tiny ones of the eye. Most of their movements are a result of our wishing them to move, and they are therefore said to be *voluntary* muscles. Study has been made of the flow of nerve impulses to and from these muscles to learn how speed, accuracy, and fatigue determine differences in skills of individuals at work, in athletics, or in other forms of bodily activity.

One of the most interesting results of this study of the nerve impulse is the light it has thrown upon the striped muscles as the seat of the kinesthetic sense receptors, and the important part these receptors play in the improvement of walking, writing, speaking, handling tools, and all other activities involving muscular movement. A blind man learning to travel familiar streets without a guide, the experienced driver easing down on his brakes to keep from skidding, a skilled workman tapping the brittle casting in a fashion to avoid breaking it, or the typist using the so-called "touch" system suggest myriads of other uses of the kinesthetic sense beyond those of mere locomotion.

Smooth muscles. The second kind of muscle, more hidden from observation and hence much less commonly known, consists of the smooth tissue found in the walls of the stomach, intestines, veins, arteries, and other internal organs. They are called *involuntary* muscles because they operate from automatic or semiautomatic controls and not as a result of our direct will. The stomach does not churn food, nor the intestines pass food along, because we wish it; these processes occur without our will. What enables the ostrich to swallow the orange or the horse to dispatch through his long esophagus the large wad of masticated hay? Smooth muscles running lengthwise along the esophagus contract in front of the object being swallowed, while rings of these tissues around the esophagus relax in front of, and contract behind, the object, thus forcing the food along its way (peristaltic movement). The expanding of the smooth muscles in the veins and arteries of the face enlarges these vessels and enables the skin to hold more blood, thereby making it look redder in blushing or in "the flushed countenance." Opposite reactions cause paleness.

Instead of the threadlike fibers of the striped muscles, which cause them to be called "striped," the smooth, or involuntary, muscles consist of tapering spindles so interwoven as to produce an unstriated, whitish tissue. The formation may be observed in the lining of the chicken's gizzard.

Facts to remember about these smooth muscles are: (a) they react mainly to emotional stimuli, (b) they react more slowly, (c) they are not under the individual's direct conscious control —that is, they are less subject to the individual's wishes or will. Everyone knows, or has been told, that laughter and pleasant associations aid digestion, whereas shocks of anger or grief take away appetite. Fear usually reaches its climax *after* some quickly occurring danger has been passed. One can flex or unflex the arm quickly and at will, but one cannot so readily or willingly blush or stop blushing.

Duct and ductless glands. Other reactors are the *duct* and the *ductless* glands. The duct glands, such as the salivary and tear glands, are well known and do not so directly influence behavior. Concerning the importance of the ductless (endocrine or internal secretion) glands and recent discoveries in this field, Poffenberger says:

"Increasing knowledge of the functions of internal secretory organs in regulating metabolism (chemical change of food into bodily energy) is shedding light upon some of the mysteries of human achievement. The capacity for meeting emergencies by sudden spurts of power, or for greatly prolonged work as a result of incentives, and for overcoming apparent exhaustion in times of great excitement, that have made our conception of fatigue seem unreal, is closely associated with the function of the *adrenal glands.* For instance, *the substance secreted by these glands (adrenalin), among other reactions, stimulates the liver to discharge its reserves of energy-producing material into the blood stream, stimulates the breathing to provide the blood with more oxygen, increases the rate at which the blood travels, and at the same time stimulates the kidneys to draw off from the blood stream the by-products of work.*" [1]

The *endocrine,* or *ductless,* gland system includes a large number of different glands, but all work in such close harmony that the function of no one seems to be totally independent of those of the others. The system, in general, governs growth, nutrition, sex, and other routine bodily functions. The *adrenal glands* are located over the kidneys; the *thyroids,* along the windpipe near the Adam's apple; the *pituitary,* at the base of the brain; and the *interstitial sex cells,* in the tissue and clustering about the reproductive cells. Common-sense observers have for many years realized that there is a connection be-

[1] Poffenberger, A. T., *Applied Psychology.* D. Appleton-Century Co., Inc.

tween sex development and type of muscular growth, voice, beard, and many personality characteristics that distinguish man from woman. Moreover, they have surmised that the sex glands furnish a secretion that brings about these developments. However, it is now known that these developments are due to the activity of another kind of cell, or ductless gland, the interstitial cell, rather than the duct glands of reproduction.

There are other ductless glands, and some organs, like the liver and pancreas, that have both duct and ductless functions. The interdependence of all the glands suggests the term "orchestra" that has often been applied to them. It should be remembered that, at present, knowledge of the exact nature and work of these glands is limited, but there can be little doubt that they have a direct and far-reaching influence on human health, endurance, and general behavior. Students interested in this subject should have little difficulty in finding additional materials if they refer to the index of almost any general textbook on psychology or biology.

STIMULUS-RESPONSE HYPOTHESIS

We have already observed that whatever happens, whether within an individual or in his environment, that causes sense receptors to transmit impulses along neurons may be called a *stimulus*. When the impulses have reached the cortex, thus creating awareness, there will normally be some sort of response.[2] A stimulus may be:

1. A direct physical force that acts upon a sense receptor (sound wave, light wave, chemical activity, pressure, etc.);

2. An indirect cause of reaction (a feeling, an appetite, an idea, etc.);

3. The *meaning* of any particular stimulus (the interpretation that the cortex has put on some prior stimulus).

[2] The study of physiology discloses that responses may also occur at two levels before impulses reach the cortex. Such first- and second-level responses are involved with reflexive behavior and automatic body-functions of survival. They are passed over in this discussion in order not to complicate the picture of third-level responses, which are more closely under our own control.

A response may be:

1. A more or less complex series of muscular moves (overt behavior);

2. A purely mental observation (analysis and classification);

3. An emotional feeling.

A workman hearing a buzzer may recognize that it means lunchtime and consequently may make a series of moves that concern leaving his work. Or he may recognize that the "boss" is wanted in the front office and go right on with his occupation. Again, he may recognize the buzzer as being the fire alarm and become so excited as to fumble in his thinking and acting. It is important to remember that the *meaning of the stimulus*[3] to the brain receiving it becomes a new stimulus that governs subsequent responses.

This stimulus-response process (extremely simplified in the foregoing account) is the mechanism used in all learning. It is the *physical* basis of habit formation. Even though science does not yet know *why*,[4] it does know that each time an impulse travels over the same combination of neurons it is easier for a succeeding impulse to travel that same neural pathway. This is particularly observable in learning any muscular technique, whether it be writing or walking or playing a musical instrument. Let the reader recall any muscular skill he may and then reflect that there was first a slow period of establishing and refining correct neural messages involved. Next there was repetition at increasing speeds until a satisfactory level of performance was reached. "Practice makes perfect," goes an old saying.

The increased speed that is developed by practicing is

[3] This process is called *perception* and receives additional study in Unit V of this book.

[4] The theory with the widest present acceptance maintains that each time an impulse traverses a given route of neurons an unexplained resistance which is supposed to exist at junction points (synapses) is reduced, thereby making the next trip by that route easier. This is known as the Synaptic-Resistance theory and has recently been the object of doubt and further investigation.

largely the result of shortening the period of interpretation and deliberation in the brain. To be sure, some of the speed may result from the reducing of resistance at given points along the neural pathway, but, in general, the speed of travel of an impulse along a neuron does not change much. The speed varies from one individual to another, from about 200 to 600 feet-per-second, with the average being about 400 feet-per-second.

This brief review of sensory, nerve, brain, muscular, and glandular equipment should serve at least to remove learning, or habit formation, from the realms of the mystical. One finds that it is indeed a physiological process. And just as one may make safe and proficient use of his car without being a skilled auto mechanic, so one may understand and apply the laws of habit formation, or personality building, without being either a physician or a technical psychologist.

Problem I
How are the sense organs involved in learning?

CASE 1

To determine whether or not rats depended upon the sense of sight in learning the short cuts to food, blind rats were run through a maze. These learned to keep out of the dead end streets just as rapidly as did normal rats. Then it was suggested that perhaps the rats were guided by the sense of smell. So the olfactory cells were removed from some of the blind rats, and again they made about as rapid progress as before. —Perhaps they felt their way around by means of their whiskers? Others were taken without sense of sight or smell and shorn of their whiskers, and again these made about the same progress in learning to run the maze as did the others.

Could this be explained in terms of the kinesthetic sense?

CASE 2

Write in the name of the sense or senses by means of which the brain becomes aware of:

1. An apple: _____
2. A beefsteak: _____
3. A handshake: _____
4. A pin-prick: _____

5. Music: _____
6. Weight: _____
7. Rocking of chair: _____
8. Hunger: _____

CASE 3

Can an individual train himself to make more useful interpretations of what his senses report to him?

1. The blind recognize their acquaintances by the sound of their voices.

2. The skilled typist never looks at the letters on the keyboard.

3. Much training is given to the eye by constant inspection. This inspection is not confined to the inspector, but it is the constant practice of workman and foreman.

4. The bricklayer develops a fineness of control that allows him to dispense with sight in some parts of his work.

5. The good trouble shooter usually knows what is wrong with the motor before he starts taking it apart.

CASE 4

A food-manufacturing plant employs a public relations man to conduct visitors on tours through the plant. He is charged with the responsibility of deciding which visitors may be taken on which tours. He investigates the visitor's interests and experience backgrounds before deciding whether to conduct tour X or tour Y. Tour X gives the visitor an impression of the size and modernness of the plant without letting him see or smell any critical chemicals or seasonings. Tour Y shows the visitor the "whole works."

Have the sense receptors anything to do with a visitor's ability to carry away trade secrets for a competitor?

What would a visitor have to have previously done with his senses in order to carry away secrets?

Problem II

How do parts of the nervous system function as parts of an electrical system?

CASE 1

By filling in the blanks show parts of the nervous system as similar in function to parts of a telephone system.

1. Transmitters: _____
2. Incoming wires: _____
3. Switchboards: _____
4. Connecting cables: _____
5. Wires going out from
   central: _____

6. Space closed by plugging in:
   _____
7. Receivers: _____
8. Electric current: _____
9. Batteries: _____

Problem III

How does acquiring muscular skill develop the brain?

CASE 1

We should think of a human individual, not as being composed of one part that carries physical activity and another very different one that does the thinking, but as a unit which both thinks and acts.

CASE 2

Few magazine articles in recent years have attracted wider attention than "If I Were 21" by William S. Knudsen,[5] a director of General Motors Corporation. "You can tell a boy what a pump is," says Mr. Knudsen, "but if he gets a pipe and, by means of a cork on a string, draws water up through that pipe, he really understands what a pump is. Even if your youngster is to be a preacher, a doctor, or a lawyer, let him spend time at manual training and mechanics. Hand training is an essential part of brain training. . . . And brain training is an essential part of hand training. The best man is one who combines the learning of books with the learning that comes of doing things with the hands. He is one who can, as Charles F. Kettering says, 'transfer the science of formula into the science of things!'"

CASE 3

The discovery of a Los Angeles psychologist, Dr. Grace Fernald, that an eleven-year-old boy (pronounced feeble-minded by his teacher because he could not be taught to read) could learn reading rapidly by being shown how to trace the letters in words with his fingers has led to new interest in learning through the kinesthetic sense. Albert E. Wiggam reviews for *Reader's Digest*[6] this method of instruction.

[5] *The American Magazine* (reprinted in *Reader's Digest*, December, 1939).
[6] "Touch and Low." *Today* (reprinted in *Reader's Digest*, December, 1936).

"The absolute-zero readers are not numerous in any school, but the very poor readers, by all estimates, constitute at least one-fourth of all pupils.

"Such children, tragically, usually are considered defective. But instead, they merely get their learning in a different way—technically the 'kinesthetic' way. Instead of learning through eyes and ears, they learn through their muscles and nerves. They learn by doing and feeling, with all their bodily senses. And thus they learn better. The memory of it goes deeper.

"One of Dr. Fernald's 'cures' was Willie J—, who had been in the state school for delinquent boys as 'incorrigible.' In five years at the school he had learned practically nothing. He could recognize his own name only when it was written 'Wm.,' and then only by the straight line under the '*m*.' Dr. Fernald showed another boy in the state school how to teach Willie by the word-tracing method. He did the job so well that Willie went through three grades in three months. He was soon sent back to his home town and became one of the finest boys in the school, instead of going on to a career of delinquency and probable crime.

"I can best describe Dr. Fernald's method by telling you of a boy I watched take the course—a seventeen-year-old lad named Donald. He had had private tutors and had been in school eleven years, but he had learned *nothing*. He could not get a job because he could not read sales slips, prices, or labels.

"First Dr. Fernald gave him an intelligence test which showed he was mentally above average. Next she told him, 'We have a way to teach you how to read and learn as well as anybody. *Nobody ever fails*. What are you most interested in?' Donald instantly replied, 'Secret Service.' Dr. Fernald wrote the words *Secret Service* in letters about three inches high. Donald traced them with his fingers perhaps 50 times and was encouraged to *think* the word.

"Finally, Donald was ready to try to write the words, and the original paper was taken away. At first he wrote 'Sert. Serc.' Dr. Fernald exclaimed, 'Fine!' Then she gave him the model again. He traced it several times. In about three hours Donald wrote *perfectly* the sentence, 'I am interested in Secret Service'—more than he had been able to do in the previous eleven years. As soon as he was able to write this sentence, the words were typed, so he could compare them with his written words. From this point Donald went tracing new words. This tracing period lasts only two or three weeks with some children; others carry it on for months or longer."

UNIT III

Learning

Objectives

1. *To develop an understanding of: (a) why people learn; (b) what the learning process is; (c) the methods people use in learning.*
2. *To develop an understanding of principles that may aid learning.*
3. *To recognize that one has the ability and the need to continue learning throughout life.*
4. *To appreciate the value of past experience as related to new learning.*

INTRODUCTION

Up to this point we have been concerned with the urges or causes of human activity and with the nerve, muscle, and gland equipment by means of which man does something about his needs. The process of discovering and improving actions that may satisfy needs is called *learning*. When the weather is too warm, people use fans, go swimming, dress lightly—try to keep cool. In winter they turn on the heat, wear woolens, install storm windows—try to keep warm. In general each individual learns from his experiences in proportion to his native capacity or natural ability. This is one reason why we say the learner must be treated as an individual. "Learning is the grindstone that sharpens the tools of inherited ability." [1]

Learning has often been defined as the *modification of behavior*. One can modify his behavior so that it is more beneficial or less beneficial to him. He can learn "good" things and "bad" things; but whether good or bad in the long run, they seemed to satisfy something in him at the time of learning.

[1] Ruch, F. L., *Psychology and Life.* Scott, Foresman & Co.

WHY PEOPLE LEARN

Learning almost always starts with an unsatisfied desire. The individual wants something he does not have. However, if the hungry man's food is immediately set before him by someone else, he has no need nor chance to learn. Consequently, there must be a blocking of satisfaction or some problem to solve.

Long before the coming of the science of psychology, preachers were saying that hardships develop character. Some common-sense observer had coined the proverb: "Necessity is the mother of invention." In other words, it has long been recognized that necessity, or felt need, is the starting point for learning. The newborn baby would probably not live if temperature discomforts did not cause it to expand its lungs in crying, or if hunger did not cause it to eat.

An unsatisfied desire and an obstacle constitute a crisis for the individual. A heightened tension drives him to some sort of activity to overcome the blocking. When the blocking has been overcome and the tension is reduced, the individual may be said to have reached an adjustment of some sort. An act of learning has been accomplished when some way around some obstacle, when some solution to some problem, has been found. A new neural pathway, or some new sets of neural pathways, have been established.

We build these new neural pathways by means of a process of interpreting the unknown in terms of the known. —What is the appearance of the western tamarack tree? One dictionary definition is: "The black larch; a North American pine." To the reader who does not know the larch, the first definition means nothing, that is, offers no familiar associations to give him a clue as to the nature of the tamarack; however, if he knows pine trees, the second definition gives him a start. Step by step the learner is told of differences between the tamarack and the pine: bark smoother and of lighter color, branches shorter and more nearly horizontal, needles shorter and paler green. These new concepts, requiring new neural pathways in the brain, are added to the old concepts, and thus we add to our total knowledge.

However, if the individual does not *want* to learn about, say, the western tamarack—does not feel some frustration at his ignorance—there will be no heightened tension nor subsequent activity and thus no learning. He can even scan the preceding data and have it virtually "go in one eye and out the other" without later knowing anything about a western tamarack.

While nature undoubtedly starts people off in life with individual differences in physique and in "intelligence," anyone far enough up the ladder of learning to be interested in these pages will observe that it is not so much what mental equipment he has inherited as *what he does* with that equipment that will help or hinder his progress. It is appropriate here for the person who wishes to increase the efficiency of his learning to consider a few basic principles that affect the learning process.

REPETITION

In the second unit of this book, the idea was discussed that repeated traversal of the same neural pathways by nerve impulses is the physical basis of habit formation. It therefore follows that the *principle of repetition* is an important principle to bear in mind in almost all learning situations. In such commonplace behavior as walking or speaking we are not conscious of the many subtle and intricately co-ordinated neural messages that are racing through the body. Repetition has made the process so mechanical that we are apt to forget that they all had to be learned with considerable difficulty at first. So it is with using a spoon at meals, or changing a quarter into nickels. Any other learning that we would like to have become "automatic" or "second nature" may become so by application of this principle of repetition.

MOTIVATION

Assuming that an individual is mature enough to learn a given technique, whether it be a child learning to lace shoes, or a new employee learning how to mix ingredients, another basic principle that is going to affect the process of learning is the degree of his interest. This principle is sometimes referred to as the *law of readiness*. If one were to state such law in words, it would read loosely like this: "The greater the degree of readiness on the part of the learner, the quicker and easier the learning." Readiness in this instance might be thought of as eagerness. If a boy is highly eager to learn the currently popular dance figures, it will not take him long to do so. We say that he is motivated. If, on the other hand, he is not very eager to learn third-conjugation endings of French verbs (only learns them because he "has to"), such learning will probably be a long, slow, arduous undertaking and probably will be of doubtful long-term success. He is clearly not much motivated.

Many factors may contribute to, or detract from, motivation. These factors are usually connected with seeking the satisfying or avoiding the unsatisfying. An animal in a puzzle box finds its way out much more quickly when it is hungry than when it is well fed—when the box is filled with ice than when it is cozy and warm. Any of the basic and secondary drives discussed in Unit I may affect eagerness. We recognize motivation as being a condition within the individual himself.

EFFECT OF ENVIRONMENT

A logical next step will bring us to another important principle: that any factor or combination of factors in the environment of the learner or the learning situation may have their effect on the degree of motivation already within the learner. The boy learning dance steps may have his eagerness dampened if his "gang" ridicules him for being a "sissy." On the other hand he may have his eagerness to learn French verbs heightened if his favorite "date" likes French and wins him to it, or if it seems as if he will be making a trip to France next summer. Imagine what will happen to the degree of interest of a new employee, who is learning how to operate a machine, if the place is so noisy that he cannot hear his trainer; or it is so dark that he cannot see what his trainer is trying to show him; or so bright that he has to squint against glare; or it is too hot or too cold; or his trainer is abusive in his correction; or, finally, the latter breathes secondhand garlic in his face. These or any other disagreeable conditions serve as distracters. They keep the learner from concentrating on what is important—the learning process. They also set up disagreeable associations with the learning, and we have already learned that any organism tends to avoid the unsatisfying.

RECOGNITION OF PROGRESS

One of the most satisfying associations a learner can have is to know that he is making progress, or better yet, to know that his progress is recognized. This is a principle which, if applied wisely, is most productive in training employees, teaching students, rearing children, or in any situation where one individual is trying to effect a modification of behavior in others. Naturally, indiscriminate "back-slapping" can defeat its own purpose. A good motto might be, "Credit where credit is due."

The foregoing discussion could be condensed into a four-statement summary of important conditions that we should keep in mind in all learning, or habit-forming, situations.

1. Repetition on the part of the learner establishes surer neural pathways.

2. Interest on the part of the learner makes the learning process quicker and easier.

3. Environmental influences may raise or lower the amount of the learner's interest.

4. Recognition of progress is an important environmental influence.

In general, those reactions that are accompanied by satisfaction are learned more readily and retained longer than reactions accompanied by annoyance, dissatisfaction, or disappointment.

It would be unfortunate if defining these particular principles of learning should give the student the impression that any one of them operates as a "law unto itself" and apart from the others. They are merely conditions that can be favorable or unfavorable to learning, and one condition alone seldom influences any act of learning. A hungry person is *motivated* to eat, and eating when hungry is *satisfying*. The worker who is doubted, criticized, or is "working in the dark" may be unable to concentrate on his task, and, in his after-work time, he may be so annoyed by disagreeable recollections that he will not spontaneously "think over" or retrace his newly formed habit paths, with the result that he fails to strengthen these pathways by repetition. These are considerations that should be kept in mind in every discussion in which the word "incentive" is used.

How Learning Is Achieved

In explaining how learning is achieved, psychologists have described three methods, or processes: (a) *trial and error,* (b) *imitation,* and (c) *logical analysis.* A close examination reveals that the three are fundamentally one. Imitation and analysis may be regarded as higher, later, and more characteristically *human* refinements of trial and error. Although this is not to say that in some of the more developed animals, such as the chimpanzee or even the dog, some use of imitation and logical analysis is not made, the usual primitive animal method of learning is by trial and error. In laboratory experiments, the cat that has learned by trial and error to work its way out of a puzzle box may unlock the door in the presence of an inexperienced cat. However, the second cat, when locked in alone, does not imitate but, instead, has to go through the same trial-and-error process as did the first. Human learning is not without its trial-and-error elements, but human beings use imitation and analysis to minimize the time and labor involved in learning. *Random trial* becomes *thoughtful, guided trial* and the errors are accordingly reduced.

Psychologists seem unable to emphasize too strongly the fact that trial must precede, or be closely associated with, all *telling* or *showing*. Unless a learner has had reasonably similar experience that he can transfer, he will be unable to grasp the operation fully from mere explanation or demonstration. Rather, he will have to go through the reactions himself. The following explanation from Vaughan clarifies this:

"It is by means of kinesthetic sensations that the movements of our own members are appreciated, involving muscles, tendons, joints, and skin. . . . When you go into a dark room and search for the light, you guide yourself by kinesthetic cues. In learning any game of skill the kinesthetic sense is highly important for getting 'the feel' of the correct motion. In golf or tennis it is difficult for the beginner to master the proper swing. Showing the pupil how you do it is of limited value. It is far more effective to let him make the swing while you guide it through the right arc. Such a procedure gives him the 'feel.' The expert is one who notices how it 'feels' to make a good stroke and then on the basis of that 'feeling' can produce another stroke of the same kind." [2]

On the other hand, trial merely for trial's sake may be overemphasized. The extent of the learner's interest and ability and the intelligent timing and wording of the instructor's suggestions are important factors in determining the *number* of trials a learner must make in acquiring mastery of a task. On relatively short unit operations, the learner with reasonably normal handwork experience is often able to perform a job correctly the first time he tries it, after hearing the carefully planned explanation and observing the demonstration. He then needs performance only for the development of speed and confidence. In such tasks as playing tennis, operating a ma-

[2] Vaughan, W. F., *General Psychology*. Doubleday, Doran and Co.

chine, etc., instruction and trial must be mixed over a much longer period of time so that muscle sense, sense of sight, and other means of learning may work together.

Learning by *imitation* is a way of having trials shortened by insights acquired consciously or unconsciously while observing a demonstration or a model product. Popularly, we say that a person "catches on" or that "a light dawns." Robinson[3] presents a vivid picture of an imaginary early ancestor of man scraping indifferently on a stick with a shell or sharp stone. He had one end rather pointed when he suddenly spied a wild animal nearby. Impulsively he threw the stick, and the sharp point pierced the animal's side and brought it down. A particularly observant bystander, comprehending what had been done, made another sharpened stick. Other progressives adopted the idea, and gradually the spear was perfected and handed down from generation to generation. Such an incident, says Robinson, may have marked the beginning of civilization —or the beginning of learning. The large element of imitation (with its shortened trial and error) is seen in this incident.

In learning by *analysis* the learner goes to the "tool crib" of his past experience and inspects his stock of "tools" to see if he has the appropriate one for the job he has to do. In other words, he is performing his trials *mentally*. If his past experiences have been wide enough, and if his arrangement of such experiences has been systematic, he may find the one that fits or explains his present problem. He has saved himself much time and effort by mental trial. Effective thinking, therefore, demands or depends upon past experience, for it is out of this storehouse of associations that useful answers to present problems must come.

The Ability of the Adult to Learn

Somewhere in the upper teens, most individuals approach the end of the process of growing up and assume increased

[3] Robinson, J. H., *The Mind in the Making.* Harper & Brothers.

responsibility for their own affairs, or, in other words, approach adulthood. This is usually the period of going to work. Even though the job that one of these beginners does may be one which he is doing for the first time, he is not usually said to be adjusting himself to change. As far as he is concerned, the work he is doing already exists. He has no old habits to break. Therefore, such learning to deal with change as he may have to do must come in later years. His ability to learn during these maturer years of his life becomes a matter of vital importance to him. What may he reasonably expect of himself if changes appear in his way of living, or in his way of making a living, ten, twenty, or thirty years later?

Developments in this field of investigation in recent years are most encouraging. Contrary to the theory generally accepted a few years ago to the effect that youth is the golden age of learning, we now know that the advantage of *experience* lies with maturer persons. Experience becomes the raw material out of which thought is fabricated. The fact that learning the new is accomplished by comparing it with the familiar in past experience may well be an inspiration to the older person, who may finally come to realize that there was a shortage of experience during his early education.

As for the old theory of plasticity of youth, Thorndike has produced experimental evidence to show that the most favorable years for learning, especially in types of problems in which reasoning from experience is a major factor, lie between the ages of eighteen and forty-five and that after forty-five the decline is very slight and very gradual. In many cases, health, purpose, past training, and mature attitudes may favor the learning of the older worker. On the other hand, bad habits that have become "second nature" and bad attitudes, especially, may handicap him.

Poffenberger, in a more recent report, sets a somewhat later age for the beginning of decline.

"The varied data which have accumulated suggests the age

of twenty to twenty-five years as the terminal period of growth, and the age of fifty to fifty-five years as the beginning of decline. . . . The level of achievement that is attained at any age is much more likely to be a question of interest and incentive than of capacity. In general, the observation of Thorndike can be recommended—that no one under forty-five years of age need refrain from trying to learn anything he wants to know or do, nor can he offer age as a legitimate excuse for not learning what he ought for any reason to learn." [4]

Another advantage claimed for the adult learner—that his problems are more realistic and broader in scope—may have to do mainly with the incentive phase of learning. Whereas the youthful student is usually studying principles that he expects to apply at some future time, the adult is usually applying principles to very intense and immediate problems upon which his advancement or his business at the time depends.

The interests of groups of mature individuals, embarked on a well-planned course of study, often pass through four rather clearly defined phases or stages. In the first place, the practical man usually enrolls with a view to learning more of the "tricks of the trade"—more ideas or skills that he can apply directly to his daily work. Next, he learns that it is a real source of satisfaction to discover fundamental principles underlying what have been to him only surface practices. In the third place, he becomes interested in the development of his own personal fund of knowledge and his personal abilities. Finally, he makes the discovery that while he has been studying with a view to improving himself in his job, he has acquired insights and abilities that extend to much wider fields of activities and interests.

THE FUTURE DEPENDS UPON LEARNING

"Reels of change are being run at such a pace that, like Alice in Wonderland, we have to run to stay in the same spot." [5]

[4] Poffenberger, A. T., *Op. cit.*

[5] Lippimann, W., *The Good Society*. Little, Brown & Co.

"When a man ceases to *become* educated, he ceases to *be* educated." [6]

"Acceleration rather than structural change is the key to an understanding of our recent economic development." [7]

Such statements have been stressed by observers for several decades. The present generation in learning to deal with change faces problems that are undoubtedly more complex than ever before because of the violent disarrangement of world affairs through wars, conflicting economic philosophies, and technological progress. The future depends upon the capacity of people to *learn* how to make the best use of technical discoveries and inventions, to appreciate the practical values in unselfishness and integrity, and to devise more effective methods of organization and management.

For example, can peoples learn how best to protect themselves in a world shrunken in size and changed in relationships because of the airplane? Can individuals learn to think of wealth in terms of produced goods rather than in terms of money? Can both workers and management learn that there is no "other side of the fence," but that the real interests of both are identical?

The industrial or business supervisor occupies a pivotal position between management and worker with respect to the learning of each. He must pass on to his workers the experience and the learning of management as these are embodied in policies. In turn, he must transmit to management the physical, mental, and emotional experiences of the workers. All learning feeds upon experience. In addition, the supervisor must provide for his own learning in the filling of his key position.

No one objective could be more important to any supervisor of the activities of other people than the ability to train himself and those under his supervision in the basic attitude of expecting change, of welcoming improvement, of being adjustable rather than static. Sound changes of process, job improvement,

[6] Baker, N. D., *The Journal of Adult Education.*
[7] *Committee on Recent Economic Changes.*

and the use of modern instructional and leadership methods are among the foremost characteristics of good supervision.

Problem I

In each case-situation, point out the key problem involved and the way in which a solution was found.

CASE 1

A local manufacturing concern had four punch presses making core laminations. In order to satisfy the minimum demand of the plant, it was necessary that these four presses work to their utmost capacity. When the maximum demand had to be met, the foreman faced the problem of overtime or of asking the plant to purchase the laminations from other companies. The situation was growing more and more unsatisfactory. Upon investigation the foreman found that two automatic punch presses could supply as many laminations as the four footpresses plus the outside purchases. He convinced the management that this was the solution of the problem. At the present time, two men working regular shifts are producing enough laminations to supply the industry.

CASE 2

"I haven't had a good smoke today! Where are the cigars?" So the coolest person at the wage dispute in the manager's office averted that worst of all explosions—an ultimatum which may require bloodshed before its maker's face can be restored.[8]

CASE 3

Dick spent most of his active life doing road work. He is unexcelled as an installer of equipment. His firm recognizes that there is none better than he. His immediate superior recently left the firm for a better position, and Dick was brought in to his desk. From the outset Dick experienced difficulty in getting started. The firm, thinking that the trouble was not Dick's fault, engaged a management consultant to help him organize his work. However, Dick still seems unable to change his slant from that of a roadman to that of a supervisor. He continues to flounder along with the ever-growing conviction that he is out of his place.

What should he do? Why?

[8] Williams, W., *The Mainsprings of Men*. C. Scribner's Sons.

Case 4

The boy sees his friend's new roadster and hears his companions praising it. The final response desired is ownership and use of a car. But note the long chain of preparatory responses: (a) goes home and mopes about in silence (no results); (b) discusses roadsters in general at the dinner table (no results); (c) asks outright for a car that will make him the equal of his fellows (no results); (d) threatens to leave home (parents seem worried but make no promises); (e) proposes to quit school and get a job (gets counterproposal that if he will earn half the price of a roadster after school and during vacations the other half will be supplied); (f) works and waits two years before the satisfying response can be made.

Problem II

Identify three learning processes and show how they are interrelated.

Case 1

Imagine an aspiring rider of wild horses trying to master the arts of horsemanship (a) by having the riding process explained to him, (b) by watching a number of rodeos, (c) by slowing up moving pictures of bucking horses so that he can analyze their movements, and (d) by memorizing such rules as "Get on his back and maintain your equilibrium!" Now if we oppose this man to a rider who has conditioned his responses to kinesthetic and equilibrium sensations by riding, on which one are you going to place your bets?

Case 2

The new gas engine in a motorboat runs smoothly for a time; then the engine begins to miss and lose power. The owner stops the boat, looks at the engine, and undoubtedly "thinks" in the sense of acting with his language organization rather than with his hands.

Then he takes out the spark plugs and cleans them. But again the engine misses. He is led to investigating the gas supply; it is sufficient. He then runs the boat to the dock, takes the magneto apart and sandpapers the points for luck. Still the miss. He next cleans the carburetor and the feed pipe. Not being successful, he opens the engine and looks at the valves. They are cool and working properly. This exhausts his own organization. He takes the boat to a local expert. The expert goes over everything in much the same way as the owner had. He then tells the owner that the engine is useless. Thereupon, the owner takes his boat back to the dock, his every act showing his depressed emotional level. At the dock he becomes infantile in his reactions, trying first this thing and then another, pushing this part, pulling that, finally giving up.

He returns to the boat after a night of rest. He starts the engine up slowly, leaning over it and watching the various parts as they work. He sees the heads of the bolts that fasten the engine to the bed moving up and down. Like a flash he stops his engine, tightens the four bolts, and rushes off to tell the expert that he is fit only to patch holes in rowboats.[9]

Problem III

How may the principles of interest and effect of environment be applied in developing attitudes favorable to learning?

CASE 1

A young man trained in publishing and printing had the funds and information to warrant his purchase of a small-town newspaper. Before announcing his plan, he spent several days in the community making the following checkup:

1. Inquiring into the desires, ambitions, and experiences of many citizens relative to their news-service needs.

2. Discussing advertising ideas and possibilities with local businessmen.

3. Asking for opinions on certain features of the services he proposed to give the community.

4. Stimulating interest, curiosity, and neighborhood expectation.

How might a production supervisor, or office manager, or sales representative apply the principles upon which the newspaperman based his actions?

CASE 2

In a widely known experiment in motivation some years ago, four groups of pupils of equal ability were selected, set to work practicing

[9] Watson, J. B., *Psychology from the Standpoint of a Behaviorist.* J. B. Lippincott Co.

addition, and their rates of progress tested at the close of the first day. For the next four days, each group was placed under a different type of control and its rate of progress tested each day.

Group 1 continued apart from the others under the usual teaching methods. At the end of the fifth day this *control* group had maintained about the same rate of progress—slightly lower on the fifth than on the first day.

Group 2 was regularly recognized, praised for its improvement, and otherwise given positive approval. Marked progress was made by these pupils on the second day and on each succeeding day until, on the fifth day, they were doing between 79 and 80 per cent better than they had done the first day.

Group 3 was regularly scolded for errors, criticized, and otherwise prodded. This group also made marked improvement on the second day, but began to fall back sharply and continued to decline until, on the fifth day, its progress was only 19 per cent above the first day.

Group 4 worked in the presence of the second and third groups but was completely ignored, neither successes nor failures being noticed. These pupils made some improvement on the second day, but, as did the third group, began to decline until, on the fifth day, their work was only 4½ per cent better than on the first day.

In commenting on this experiment, Prescott says: "The results showed that regardless of age, initial ability, or sex, praise resulted in the best work, reproof was initially effective but soon lost its value, while ignoring a group left it to achieve the least." [10]

Case 3

A foreman approached a new employee whose job was to list large quantities of small articles by numbers in tabular form. The foreman's procedure was somewhat as follows:

1. Leisurely inspection of the work.
2. "I see those '7's' are clearing up—at first they looked like '2's'."
3. In a tone of happy relief, the employee flashed back, "But that '3' isn't quite clear, either, is it?"
4. "That's right," the foreman replied, "it does look a little like an '8'—don't start the loop so near the center."

---

[10] Prescott, D. A., *Emotion and the Educative Process.* American Council on Education.

Problem IV

1. *Why is a forward-looking or positive attitude toward change difficult?*

2. *Why is such an attitude of open-mindedness necessary under modern conditions?*

CASE 1

In 1900, somewhat fewer than a million persons were employed in the carriage and wagon industries in this country, as manufacturers, drivers, draymen, livery stable managers, blacksmiths, etc. In 1930, the automobile, based on innumerable scientific discoveries and engineering developments, had provided employment for 2,409,394 individuals, exclusive of those involved in oil production. These figures have been corrected for the increase in population. They show that while the advent of the automobile produced technological unemployment among carriage and harness makers, the net result for labor has been a 250 per cent increase in jobs. Early in 1940, W. J. Cameron, of the Ford Motor Company, said: "The use of the automobile and its servicing employs 6,380,000 persons." Other new industries, unknown a generation or so ago but now furnishing employment to millions, are the electrical, telephone, motion picture, radio, mechanical refrigeration, airplane, rayon, nylon, plastics, and machine tool industries.

CASE 2

Elliott Dunlap Smith shows that unchecked ruts, habits, or biases lead to stagnation, the hardening of the capacity to learn, and increasing difficulty in the making of new viewpoints. "This habit-slavery," says Dr. Smith, "is the more powerful because it is unknown. Stubborn stagnation is particularly an industrial disease. Men come into industry young. Men who become executives stay long in the same factory, often in the same department. In the normal routine of their work, factory men are sheltered from outside points of view. Life in industry is strikingly regular. Within a department men are often cloistered from the broader industrial world, as monks in a monastery were cloistered from the world about them." [11]

CASE 3

A young farmer was driving a heavy truck load of barley down a very steep and treacherous grade. Four helpers were riding on the

[11] *Psychology for Executives.* Harper & Brothers.

loaded truck. His brakes gave way; his helpers leaped out. He might have spent precious seconds cursing the brakes, wishing he had not attempted the hill, wondering why he had ever purchased so rough a farm, or otherwise looking backward or indulging in wishful thinking. What he actually did was to look ahead to a heavy clump of small trees and underbrush, into which he turned his truck. He thus saved his own life and even the truck and the load of barley from destruction.

CASE 4

A hundred years ago, the factory for making shoes consisted largely of an old tanbark mill driven by horses, and a series of vats dug in the ground and filled with water and ground tanbark for curing the hides. The equipment and personnel consisted of a few wooden forms, iron lasts, needles, sewing-thread, knives, and a shoemaker and his helper. As time went on, separate machines were built for each operation in the making of a shoe, so that now the shoe is hardly touched by hand. The human being cannot develop new hands, muscles, glands, and fingers to keep pace with civilization, but each new demand should find him still plastic and capable of forming the habits necessary to enable him to meet such demand.

CASE 5

"Rapidly changing conditions and increasing competition for executive positions resulting from the elimination of such jobs by mergers and consolidations seriously threaten the future of those executives who, through their continued adherence to 'fundamentalist' principles in their work, are not prepared to fit into the new order of business.

"The answer to 'How can I hold my job?' is 'I must prepare myself to meet the requirements of a fast-changing business world whose executives must be students of economics, history, and business administration, which together help to develop an analytical turn of mind. In turn, I must develop my ability to select, train, and guide others rather than just be a boss.'" [12]

CASE 6

In the preface to his comprehensive book, *Personnel Management and Industrial Relations*, Dale Yoder paints this word picture of the present status of human relations:

"The whole field of industrial relations is highly dynamic. Under

[12] Donald, W. J., *American Management Association Reports.*

such circumstances, the most essential characteristic of effective personnel administration is its constant self-appraisal and evaluation. Policies and practices must be constantly scrutinized and weighed in terms of their appropriateness and effectiveness. The continual testing of each phase of the industrial relations program, as a basis for constant readjustment, innovation, and adaptation, is the elementary requisite of a satisfactory program in these years of rapid change." [13]

[13] Yoder, Dale, *Personnel Management and Industrial Relations*. Prentice-Hall, Inc.

UNIT IV

Remembering

Objectives

1. *To develop an understanding of how remembering depends upon learning.*
2. *To recognize the relationship of forgetting to learning.*
3. *To develop ways of improving remembering.*
4. *To appreciate the value of past experience in constructing associations useful for remembering.*

INTRODUCTION

On a balmy western summer afternoon, an aged man was sitting on his porch a mile and a half from the banks of the Columbia River. Turning thoughtfully to a reporter who was living with him at the time, he said, "That whistle sounds to me just like the old *Belle of Memphis* on the Mississippi that I heard so much as a boy." The reporter later inquired at the offices of the company owning the river boat and learned that the whistle was indeed the same one that the elderly man had heard half-a-century earlier in his life. The *Belle of Memphis* had been dismantled many years before, and the parts shipped around the Horn and subsequently used in building the Columbia River stern-wheeler.

What is memory? A term which comes most frequently and glibly to the tongue of many people is *the subconscious mind*. It seems romantic to visualize some fictitious chamber where suppressed ideas are penned up, active, and striving to get themselves expressed. But even the novice begins to suspect the absurdity of this idea of a distinct entity if he asks himself

49

where this subconscious chamber could be located, and what could be the meaning of "an idea *active* in the subconscious."

"The Spotlight of Attention"

Perhaps there is another and more reasonable hypothesis. All the experiences of one's past life are assumed to have left their imprints in some form in one's brain. When the "spotlight of attention" is turned upon any given pattern of past experiences, those experiences are conscious and those ideas are active. As the burglar with his flashlight enters the darkened room, he shifts the light from place to place, looking for the safe. When his light is shining directly upon a certain space on the wall, that space is vividly lighted; the areas immediately surrounding this spot are light, but not as much as the center. Other more remote parts of the room may not be visibly affected at all by the shaft of light. It seems that this is analogously true of past experiences. Those upon which the spotlight of attention is immediately directed are vivid, others are in the margin of attention, while still others are totally dark or not affected by the light.

This analogy of the spotlight on the wall of a darkened room is useful if we bear in mind that it *is* only an analogy. The imprints that past experiences have left in the brain are neural pathways, or different "hook-ups" of some of the 14 billion neurons in the brain. An impression was made when a new idea was first formulated; an impulse traveled through a new neural pathway; something was learned. If the idea in question is not now being thought, no impulse is going through that particular "hook-up," so we may say that it is in the dark. If the individual directs his attention to the idea, or if something happens that directs his attention to it, then an impulse travels over the appropriate network of neurons. We may speak of this activity as "directing the spotlight of attention into the darkened area." Therefore, it may also be inferred that an idea itself is not retained at all—has no existence—when the neural connections that reproduce it are not in or near the "spotlight of attention." The thing that *is* retained is a set of nerve connections, which must be restimulated in order to bring the corresponding idea back to life. This re-established pattern of images may be called *memory*.

EXPERIENCE AND MEMORY

What were some of the elements in the story of the steamboat whistle that caused that sound to remain through life in the old man's memory? The landing of a steamboat in pioneer St. Louis *meant* something—especially to an imaginative boy who looked forward to the excitement of its coming. There were the crowds at the landing, strangers, cargoes being unloaded and loaded, dreams of travel. *Belle of Memphis* was a pleasing name, and this boat was the first one with which the boy became acquainted; he compared other boat whistles with its whistle. It will be seen here that factors aiding future recognition of the whistle were interest, clearness of first impression, and a background of associated experiences.

In the previous unit, mention was made of learning about the western tamarack in terms of comparison with the already familiar pine. How long the new associations with the word *tamarack* will stay in the learner's mind depends upon such factors as his past experience with, or interest in, timber, his future travel or property plans, whether he thinks over or renews the new connections, and, to quite an extent, his natural retentiveness.

Scientific authority and common sense agree that there are individual differences in the degree of natural retentiveness. John Dewey says, "The mere learner is not a thinker. A further condition is requisite, namely, a natural fertility of associations, i.e., the kind of mind which automatically supplies ideas bearing upon the problem. This fertility of ideas is an individual gift and, in its highest form, clear genius." The old Oregon Trail in most places has long since faded from view. But at one point, at least, the old ruts worn by the oxcarts cut deeply into the soil—soil that was held firmly in place by the matted roots of Buffalo grass. Over the sandy ridges less than a mile away, however, all signs of travel would frequently be lost before even the next company of pioneers came that way. Just as one soil holds the tracks longer than another soil, so one mind may hold learning easier than another. This does not mean, however, that any normal person cannot *improve* on the memory with which nature has endowed him.

IMPROVEMENT OF REMEMBERING

The principles which govern remembering are identical with those of learning. Learning refers to the gaining of knowledge, skills, or emotional attitudes; remembering refers to the degree in which those modifications of behavior are retained, or can be recalled by the learner. If learning is the establishing of new neural networks, remembering is the recrossing of those same networks at a later time.

Repetition. There is no doubt about the usefulness of the principle of repetition. Whether scientists prove in the long run that learning is due to the formation of habit paths through synaptic centers or to the chemical modification of brain cells, or both, or to some other brain change, it is certain that the more frequently and meaningfully an experience is rehearsed, the longer it will be retained.

Clear understanding. One of the most common faults of the learner is to let pass a problem discussed or directions received when they are only vaguely or dimly understood. Even from the purely practical standpoint of saving time and energy, one cannot afford to allow timidity, indifference, or the hope that he will "see it later" prevent his getting the clearest possible understanding of an issue. To see to it that the learner *does* understand is also the duty of the instructor or the supervisor giving orders or instructions.

Association. Then there is the vital matter of the formation of as many associational ties as possible. The forester who wants to be able to move more quickly and easily from point to point in his fire-patrol territory builds roads and trails connecting those points. The man who wants to be able to recall readily certain names or facts connects those names and facts with other things which are more easily thought of, and which, because of the associations established, will direct his attention to the names or facts he wishes to recall.

When any one sight, sound, odor, or other stimulus brings to mind other experiences of the past, these present and past responses are said to be *associated*. It does not seem necessary, for practical purposes, to enter into the debatable question of just how the association fibers of the central nervous system are connected in the formation of these associations. Whatever the nature of these nerve pathways may be, it is certain that they are strengthened or made more permanent by repetition.

The facts of learning by association are easily observed by the layman when once his attention has been called to them. For example, a certain man says he seldom hears the word "inspection" without recalling a friendly inspector who, over twenty years ago, was always helpful with instructions that the supervisor of the job had failed to provide. When two, or as is more commonly the case, a large number of experiences—factual, emotional, or what not—are encountered by the individual at the same time, the thought of one tends to bring back the others.

Similarity, contrast, and novelty may help make a game of this matter of building associations. If the name to be recalled is Whitehead, note the man's hair. If it is white, there is association by similarity; if it is black, there is association by contrast. In employing novelty, the bolder the imagery the better. One does not need to tell the other fellow of the possibly fantastic nature of the associations thrown around his name. Conscious effort in the formation of concrete associations will bring surprising results. In learning a twelve-point pledge, a candidate associated points two through eleven with the shape, size, and position of his fingers and thumbs. Having no trouble with the first and the last, he was then able to recall the rest in their proper order.

Muscular action. Certain sayings, well known in training circles, suggest a special and very practical phase of association: "We learn to do by doing." "Reactions should be learned as nearly as possible in the way in which they are to be used." "Motor and emotional reactions are as intimately tied up in the associational systems as are the purely mental operations." By considering these in the light of the observed fact that motor habits seem to be retained much longer than the purely mental, as pointed out in Units II and III, one will readily conclude that we should employ muscular action in learning, whenever it is possible to do so. The process of carving a fowl will be remembered much better if one actually carves than if one uses no muscles in the learning. If a name is to be remembered, speak it aloud, write it out.

Incentives. Rewards, recognition, knowledge of progress made, and other satisfactions come under the heading of incentives. Attention and concentration are obviously greater when the learner is interested. The same is true when he is free from distracting influences. This is but to invoke again two of the principles useful in learning that were discussed in Unit III—interest on the part of the learner, and the effect of the environment.

Confidence. The next suggestion offered is one that is less easily managed. It is confidence in one's ability to remember. While it is easy to say, "Have confidence in your memory," confidence is not so easily or simply acquired. However, confidence is a *habit* and therefore can be learned or strengthened. Confidence is of immeasurable benefit in that it saves the "spotlight of attention" from being focussed on doubts and fears and instead permits it to be concentrated upon the thing that needs to be remembered.

The foregoing six principles offer ways for the human being to do something to improve his remembering, regardless of the degree of natural retentiveness he may have inherited. Personal effectiveness depends upon recalling, at the right time, checks on performance, due dates, promises, engagements, and all other obligations and opportunities. If one is in a position of responsibility for others and for their effective performance, he will find the above principles useful for helping those others, as well as himself, to remember.

Before leaving the subject of remembering, brief attention should be given to three laws that come in for a good deal of scientific study—the laws of recency, contiguity, and intensity. This book passes them over casually for the reason that they are so apt to be merely incidental or accidental. *If* an occurrence has been *recent*, one can remember it better. *If* two ideas occurred *together* (i.e., in contiguity), they tend to be remembered together. (This is a sort of accidental association.) *If* a situation was sufficiently *intense*, it is remembered ever so long without the need to employ repetition, association, or other useful technique. It will be readily seen that these three possibilities are not under an individual's own control and therefore cannot be integrated into his own program of remembering techniques. However, knowing that they are effective, a teacher, a parent, or a supervisor might utilize them in getting other people to remember things.

Forgetting, for the practical purposes of this course of study, is the apparent inability of the mind to "shoot the juice" through the particular network of neurons that will reproduce a given idea. The causes can be many and complex, such as the recency, or the intensity, of some ideas foreign to the one wanted; or it may be any of the multitude of emotional blockings that it is the aim of psychiatry to uncover. However, the commonest cause for forgetting, or, at least, the one about which an individual can do something corrective, is merely the failure to retrace the network, or to establish it clearly in the first place. Then when the "spotlight of attention" tries to illuminate that network, the latter is submerged far beneath a welter of more recent, more intense, more clearly understood, and more frequently repeated ideas.

One final suggestion: don't clutter the mind with nonessentials. The most constructive means of being sure that certain items are properly handled is to write them down where they can be referred to and checked off at the appropriate time. If we consign to paper the routine details that can be disposed of thus, then the mind is more free to organize those experiences and impressions that broaden our judgments and aid us in solving problems. Furthermore, the use of notes, date books, and other such devices is better than the hard falls of forgetting. A well-known executive says that the study of this topic should be worthwhile, if only to emphasize the importance of developing systematic habits of getting *into writing* all promises or other obligations that cannot be immediately fulfilled. In that way they will be taken care of at their proper times, and in the form in which they were outlined at the time they were contracted.

Problem I

How does one benefit by a rich background of experience and ideas in problem solving?

CASE 1

As the hostess gives her dining table a final appraising glance, many things flash through her mind. Is the service properly appointed? Are the courses ready in the kitchen in proper sequence? Has the seating of the guests been tactfully planned? Mrs. Wilbur's yellow gown will clash with the colors her neighbor wears, and a reseating is imperative. Has the choleric Colonel Blair composed his quarrel with Mr. Nesbit? All this and more is done during the flash of an eye, but in the same tense moment we may be sure that neurons to the number of countless millions are all busy transmitting their messages hither and yon throughout the entire cortex as now one and then another associational pattern is momentarily activated.[1]

CASE 2

If a steel manufacturer hears the prices of a long list of steel products, he has little difficulty in remembering them because he com-

[1] Herrick, C. J., *The Brains of Rats and Men.* University of Chicago Press.

pares them with cost figures, thinks out what profits he can make at these prices, compares them with last year's prices at this time, estimates what the future trend of the market will be, and in a variety of ways forms associations in his mind between these figures and his well-established recollections. The same man may experience great difficulty in remembering facts concerning lumber or pottery, because in those fields the possible associations in his mind for the new facts are few. Thus in a sense people have "memories," not a general memory.[2]

CASE 3

In meeting some production difficulty, it is not necessary to be able to remember just what happened in some similar case in the past, or even to remember that a similar case happened at all. In dealing with factory discipline it is not essential to be able to repeat a rule or definition. Often people who can cite instances and repeat rules the best are the poorest in handling actual problems. There is thus a distinction between a good specific memory of particular events and·words and well-remembered understanding of a subject, a trade, or a process. . . . There are men with remarkable "Indian memories" and wide experience who always stay operatives. The memories of such men are mere storehouses of unassimilated images that are not organized into an available body of knowledge.[3]

Problem II

Explain and illustrate from your own experience the extent to which remembering depends upon the way things are learned. How would you apply the principle of learning by association to a problem of teaching an employee confidence in himself, in his job, in you, or in the company?

CASE 1

Mr. X stands in front of his home late at night and cannot get in. He has forgotten the key, and he decides that this shall not happen to him again. He takes his handkerchief and carefully ties one of the four corners into a large knot. This is to remind him of the key tomorrow.

Mr. X knows nothing about psychology, but the course of action

[2] Smith, E. D., *Op. cit.*
[3] *Ibid.*

that he follows here is perfectly correct psychologically and also effective. The following morning while he is dressing he will see the knot and immediately the image of the key will arise in his mind.

But how can the view of the knot evoke the thought of the key when there certainly is no physical resemblance between the knotted formation in the handkerchief and a key?

Let us think of a phonograph record. Upon its surface, tones of music are deposited in fine grooves. In the rendition, these tones are not thrown into a promiscuous disorder, but appear in exactly the same order as they were received.

Similarly, the occurrences that are imbedded in the brain do not awaken in any confused order, but come back to life in about the same sequence as they first passed through the consciousness.

CASE 2

Mr. Mok: Can an infant be cured of acquired fears?

Dr. Poffenberger: Yes, but it is a difficult job. A single experience may establish one of these fears, but it takes dozens of trials to rid a child of one. Once a mechanism by which the fears are acquired is understood, they can be removed by practically the same process. We call that *reconditioning or deconditioning the child.* Take, for example, the baby that is afraid of a furry rabbit. Suppose that this child is fond of a particular breakfast food; say oatmeal. The method is to bring the fearsome object in the baby's vicinity whenever it is eating this cereal. But it has to be done gradually. If it is done too quickly, it may have the opposite effect; the baby may get afraid of its food, and you would have two fears on your hands instead of one. So, the first time, the rabbit is kept at a considerable distance from the baby's chair, but each time after that, it is brought a little closer. By and by, the infant begins to hook up the rabbit with the pleasant sensation of eating oatmeal, and the fear is overcome.

Mr. Mok: Do grown people acquire their abnormal fears in the same manner?

Dr. Poffenberger: Yes, essentially the same mechanism works in adults, and is responsible for some nervous disabilities. This came out clearly in cases of shell shock during the First World War. The men were treated by keeping them absolutely quiet at a hospital. This was needed because even the dropping of a book would cause them to react violently. It often happened that a patient who was getting along pretty well suddenly would suffer a relapse, and again show all of his original symptoms—sweating, tremors, temporary paralysis. At first, the reason for such setbacks was a mystery. Then it was discovered that a man in uniform had walked through the ward. The mere sight of the soldier was sufficient to bring on a renewed attack, because the patient's original experience had been connected with men in uniform. In other words, the patient's extreme fear of a harmless doughboy was a conditioned reflex. Do you understand that the mechanism which caused him to fear the man in uniform, who was in no way responsible for his trouble, was essentially the same as that which caused the baby in Watson's experiment to fear the rabbit, though it was a noise and not the rabbit that had originally frightened it? [4]

During World War II, the term *exhaustion* largely replaced *shell shock,* and men who were given rest, relief, and treatment near enough to front lines to be within hearing of gunfire responded, it is reported, better than those given the same care in more remote base hospitals.

Problem III

Formulate a set of principles that you feel you can rely upon in improving your own memory or the memory of one whom you are training.

Case 1

"My fingers are all thumbs whenever Miss X comes near me," cried a young waitress pleading with a parent to let her quit her job. "I can work rapidly and have no trouble when I'm alone, but when she begins to tell me to hurry, to be careful, not to drop things, or that people are waiting, I start doing everything she tells me not to do. I can take care of twice as many tables when she is away and not be half as tired as when she is around watching me."

Case 2

"Curve of learning" and "curve of forgetting" are names given to lines illustrating the rate of acquiring, and the rate of losing, information. Just as learning is usually more rapid at first and then gradually levels off, so the curve of forgetting falls rapidly immediately after the learning. Every repetition of things learned promptly after the learning causes the curve of forgetting to drop less rapidly. Repetition, or periodical review, from the time of the happenings,

[4] *Popular Science Monthly.*

is probably the main reason that older folks tend to retell the same stories of their early lives. They keep their old "chestnuts" well polished through use.

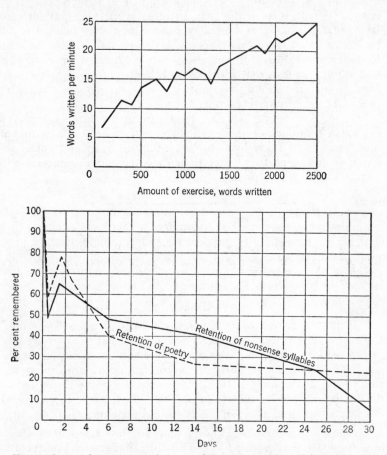

Fig. 2. Curve of Learning and Curve of Forgetting. Adapted from Moss, *Applications of Psychology*, by permission of Houghton Mifflin Company.

CASE 3

A young man took charge of a small department under most favorable circumstances. The superintendent thought he had a "find" in him. A few weeks later this superintendent, when asked how his young foreman was getting along, said: "There is just one thing wrong with him—he won't ask enough questions when a job is being given him to be sure he understands it thoroughly. I don't know whether he is afraid he will seem dumb, or whether he just hopes he understands it well enough to get by. But often he comes back with something done wrong. He surely could not forget if he clearly understood explanations made when the jobs were being taken over."

CASE 4

The lecture method of teaching probably grew up because it represents the least effort for the teachers, but it is being superseded by the discussion method because of the greater permanence of understanding and knowledge gained through participation on the part of the learners. For much the same reason, laboratory methods are used wherever possible. "Put the learner through the reaction" is a well-known phrase in discussions of teaching on the job.

CASE 5

A young politician used carefully prepared notes during his first few addresses; however, when he was ready to appear again on the platform, he found that he was unable to locate his briefcase. In a resigned state of mind, he went ahead and found that he was able to make the best speech of his career by depending entirely upon his memory to bring forth his arguments. He never needed, or used, notes again.

CASE 6

A college president, with a reputation for remembering students' names, regularly called freshmen into his office and talked with them. What association devices may he have used?

CASE 7

A certain executive has announced to his associates that in the future no alleged promise will be honored unless it has been made in writing. He is attempting to get all obligations placed on record. In many factories this motto is widely circulated: "Don't say it; write it." More and more foremen are acquiring the habit, as they go through their departments, of taking notes of requests made of them; or a foreman will ask those who make requests to write them and put them on his desk.

UNIT V

Reliability of Judgment

Objectives

1. To organize for practical review definite facts and principles that bear upon the formation of sound judgment, especially where quick decisions must be made.
2. To practice checking causes of bad snap judgments and the formation of better ones.
3. To encourage the practice of open-mindedness, suspended judgment, or a scientific attitude in dealing with problem situations.

INTRODUCTION

A few years ago the Buffalo *News* printed this hunter's epitaph:

> "Beneath the weeping willow tree lies
> Edward Everett Bier,
> Who, by another hunter, was mistaken
> for a deer."

It would seem as if someone in such a case would be guilty of misjudgment, that is, faulty perception. That "someone" thought he saw a deer; he was so sure of it that he discharged a firearm. Was the cause of this "mistake" poor vision? Or is it possible that the mind can play tricks on us? We need to look at that process in human behavior which psychologists call *perception*.

Let's review for a moment some material on the nervous system. We know, for instance, that whatever occurs in our environment that the sense receptors can report to the cortex is called a stimulus. If we have a combination of several stimuli, the combination is often referred to as a *stimulus situation*.

62

When a stimulus situation occurs, the appropriate sense receptors and neurons send appropriate impulses to the cortex, and
the cortex becomes *aware* of the stimulus situation. Now, in the
cortex we give *some kind of meaning* to the message we have
received. We interpret it—or "make something" of it.

Sometimes one realizes that he is having difficulty in making an interpretation. When he hears a strange sound, or seems
to smell something burning in his car, or sees someone behaving in a peculiar way, he is apt to ask of someone else, "What do
you make of that?" He is seeking the aid of another mind to
help him arrive at a *perception*. On such occasions, one is conscious of the fact that there is a process of arriving at a conclusion. However, in the vast majority of cases, people arrive almost instantaneously at their conclusions and are therefore not
conscious that there is such a process.

PERCEPTION

We can set down a useful formula if we allow *A* to stand for
awareness, *I* for *interpretation*, and *P* for *perception*:

$$A + I = P$$

Awareness plus interpretation is perception.

"We *sense* the physical world; we *perceive* what it means.
. . . The two steps sometimes stand out separately, even in
everyday experiences. Is the faint noise we hear the sound of
an airplane in the distance, or of an automobile, or of a gaso-
line boat, or the buzz of a fly? Is this farm implement a potato-
digger, a fertilizer-spreader, or a tobacco-planter? Such lags in
our mental processes cause us to realize that the act of perception is not complete until a convincing interpretation, right or
wrong, has been made." [1]

In the quotation above, the words "right or wrong" are of interest to the student of human behavior. Psychologically, a perception has been made when the mind puts its own interpreta-

[1] Tiffin, J., Knight, F. B., and Asher, F. J., *The Psychology of Normal People.*
D. C. Heath & Company.

tion on some stimulus situation. Now, what we are concerned with is how to make these judgments more reliable. How may we avoid the traps that lure us into having false perceptions? It is often far more than a joke to "see" in the pair of shoes under the bed an armed burglar. How easy it is to interpret the manager's hurrying through the department without speaking as an impending shutdown or bankruptcy. If an employee is summoned to the front office, he may easily conclude that he is going to be bawled out or laid off.

Practically every set of rules for supervision includes caution against hasty judgment or, in other words, urges getting the facts before making a decision. But those in positions of leadership are not the only ones who need to study their own conduct with a view to improving judgment. Wise judgment saves the shopper from wasting her funds on poor materials, the hunter from injuring his friend, or the worker from quitting the very job that may hold for him his greatest advancement. It is the aim of this unit to enable the reader or the discussion group to set up a score card of common causes of error— to become conscious of where we most often find pitfalls to wise judgment.

PRINCIPAL INFLUENCES

One of the basic facts that everyone should understand about off-hand judgments is that their accuracy depends fully as much upon *the person passing judgment* as upon *the thing judged*. This is perfectly logical when we remember that the judgment is really a perception, and that a perception is in a person's mind—not outside of the person in some inanimate object. Returning, then, to the equation $A + I = P$, we can see that if one wants reliable perception, he must first have reliable awareness and reliable interpretation. The main influences determining the soundness or unsoundness of an individual's awareness may be outlined under three main headings: bodily conditions, experience, and mental set.

1. BODILY CONDITIONS

1. *Limitations of the sense receptors* often prevent the mind's really getting a very accurate sensation. If this were not so, the grocer would not need his scales; the surveyor, his measuring tape; the singer, his pitch pipe; nor the heating engineer, his thermometer. Fashion experts know how to arrange the lines in clothes to make the short person look taller and the tall look shorter. "All that glitters is not gold," is a familiar saying indicating common-sense recognition that our sense receptors are by no means infallible. If they were, there would be no bookings for sleight-of-hand performers.

2. *Health* colors the entire perceptive process. It can affect the way in which the sense receptors report a sensation, and it can affect the way the individual weighs that sensation in his thinking process. The foreman or teacher may easily see in the youthful questioner either impudence or interest, according to the state of his own digestion. It hardly seems reasonable that intelligent men and women should take their headaches, indigestion, or fatigue into their work or other social relationships, and pass on the results of their ailments to others; yet many admit—almost brag—that they do just that, and they imply in their admissions that they probably will continue to do so.

2. EXPERIENCE

1. *Specific experiences* accumulate during a person's life to make up his total experience. The present and the future are judged by the past because one can think only in terms of the neural networks already established when trying to form new ones. If we were trying to find the reason for a new and peculiar sound in an automobile engine, how reliable would be the judgment of a person who had never heard automobile engines before?

Not all of a person's past experience comes because it was always his specific aim to learn particular material; much of it comes incidentally and almost unobserved. Many emotional attitudes have this kind of background. "Some grown men are afraid of cats, running water, lightning, and drafts. By very detailed examination and analysis, it can be shown that every single thing which we now do as adults can be traced directly back to things that occurred last year, five years ago, or twenty years ago." [2] In his play, his study, and his work, each individual is building experience (i.e., accumulating specific experiences) with materials and people that will help him in arriving at future perceptions.

It is through this almost unconscious method in everyday dealing with people that the ability to judge human nature is acquired. Judging human reactions is learned through contacts with people, and one does not always know just how he makes his judgments. *Cues* leading to correct conclusions often lie just outside of the focused attention of the person doing the thinking. Mind reading is largely muscle reading. Man often gives woman credit for possessing *intuition*—supposedly some innate insight—when in reality she has only learned through constant human contact to observe keenly the many faint and fleeting evidences or signs of personal traits or attitudes.

2. *Logic* is usually defined as the science of orderly and accurate thinking. Lack of proper training in straight thinking is a most frequent cause of errors in judgment. Inductive logic is the cornerstone of modern science; it demands that we hold up our decisions until enough evidence is at hand to warrant a safe conclusion. Every jury is charged with the responsibility of withholding judgment until sufficient evidence has been submitted to permit of a verdict accurate "beyond a reasonable doubt." This is the very opposite of forming hasty conclusions, and is what is meant by *open-mindedness*, or the *scientific attitude*.

Josh Billings had in mind the popular lack of logical think-

[2] Rosenstein, J. L., *Human Relations for Executives*. McGraw-Hill Book Co., Inc.

ing when he said that people know too many things that "ain't so." He gave as example a long list of common beliefs, such as: "all minister's sons are wild; all Chinese smoke opium; all redheads have quick tempers." One can easily furnish other examples of this all-too-common practice of drawing conclusions without sufficient evidence. This error has been called *the fallacy of the dramatic instance*. Self-training in logical thinking should not be difficult if the individual watches himself and practices conscientiously such common-sense philosophy as "be sure you're right, then go ahead." During World War II, *Job Relations Training* emphasized this with its "four-step method"—get the facts; weigh and decide; take action; follow up.

3. MENTAL SET

1. *Attitudes* are tendencies to react in a certain fashion. It was the hare's attitude that caused him to lose the race with the tortoise. On the other hand, it was the attitude of the tortoise that caused him to win. Attitudes may often bring a less talented person a greater success.

To find the origin of some attitudes one might have to trace his experience back through a number of years. However, some other attitudes may be formed rather immediately. These latter are usually connected with what seems to be important to an individual's security at the time. The story is told of a young woman who was for several years an active agitator, lecturer, and writer on behalf of communism. She then entered an essay contest and won $5,000. Overnight she lost all desire to "share the wealth."

What can we do about our attitudes? Well, they are *learned;* hence, if we want to strengthen one, we must practice it. If we want to unlearn an attitude, we can replace it by practicing a different one. This is simply habit formation.

2. *Expectation* is a condition of mind wherein one sabotages his own observation and logic. Instead of letting a *stimulus* lead to a *response* in the normal fashion, he gets a

response all set up in the mind prematurely. It is so *ready* to happen that he doesn't even need the whole stimulus to start the response. The hunter, referred to at the beginning of this unit, so *expected* a deer to arrive that he shot another hunter instead. Expectation can indeed produce such strong mental images that serious physical alterations may follow.

A teacher of prominence was driving through Massachusetts one August day when he saw some tempting blueberries by the roadside. He stopped his car, climbed through the fence, and ate some of the berries. A few moments later he saw by the roadside a sign which read: "These berries are sprayed with arsenic." Almost immediately he felt a dryness and burning in the throat. He speeded up, and by the time he reached the nearest village he was in actual pain. He rushed into a drugstore, told the druggist what he had done, and asked for an antidote. Thereupon he learned that the berries had not been sprayed at all—that the sign was up merely as a protection against tourists.

3. *Desire* is closely related to expectation, but it is such a severe offender in causing false judgments that it deserves special mention. Here again the mind arranges a perception in advance, but this time it is the perception that we *desire* to have, whether or not it matches up to the realities of the situation. We don't even *see* the faults in our friends; we don't see any virtue in our foe. The condition described here does not refer to those situations where there is conscious distortion of facts, that is, purposeful deceit. It refers rather to situations where one's interpretation is *really confused* by what his wishes are. Mama *knows* that Junior did not tip the neighbor's baby out of its carriage; he just happened to be standing by the carriage when the baby threw its weight.

The above discussion furnishes an outline of areas in which to watch for perceptual pitfalls:

1. *Bodily conditions:*
  (a) Limitations of the sense receptors.
  (b) Health.

2. *Experience* (*total*):
   (a) Specific experiences.
   (b) Logic.
3. *Mental set:*
   (a) Attitudes.
   (b) Expectation.
   (c) Desire.

These areas are not actually as distinctly defined as their listing here would indicate. It does not require much imagination to see that health can color a mental set; that expectation can distort logic; that the limitation of a sense receptor can create a desire; etc. Whatever may be the cause of false perception, it is usually located by searching for the weak practices or limitations of the observer.

A very practical fact that requires consideration, especially in a course in dealing with people, is that personal bias, personal health, and personal experience are likely to warp judgments about *people* more readily than they warp judgment about things. We live in what is called a "social" age. From nursery school to the end of school life the child is concerned with teacher-student relationships, athletic teams, social clubs, and many other human situations. Later in life he has relationships with bosses, associates, relatives, friends, neighbors, and a multitude of others. Since *emotion* is an ever present, explosive element making greater the danger of misjudging people, the habit of checking on causes of error in social perception should be of tremendous value.

Whether or not geography is concerned in it, we all know what is meant by the saying, "I'm from Missouri." Before jumping to a conclusion, the man "from Missouri" would examine his own understanding of the problem at hand; he would question his breadth of experience; he would examine his attitudes; he would guard against prejudice, desire, or expectation. If he were considering a problem requiring measurement he could not guess, he would measure. If he were drawing conclusions from data, he would seek the aid of statistics.

This may all seem like a great deal of trouble, but *correct habits,* once formed, *work rapidly with a minimum of resistance.* In the long run one is repaid many times for the pains he has taken in self-discipline. Missteps are costly: a single one may prove a man's downfall. The road to improvement lies in (a) understanding the nature of the pitfalls that exist, and (b) constructing new habit paths around the points of greatest weakness.

Problem I

What is perception? Where is judgment likely to be more accurate—in material or in human situations?

Case 1

If a foreman looks at a machine, he actually sees only one side. Though much of what is essential is hidden, he provides what he cannot see from his memory. Moreover, his memory automatically adds to the machine its various attributes. Though the machine may be standing motionless, he perceives the motor as capable of power, some parts as stationary, and others as movable. Though the machine may be painted, he recognizes some parts as steel and some as brass and adds to each metal its properties.[3]

Case 2

If a man is blunt, he speaks of things that make his audience gasp; if he is tactless he talks or acts to the injury of his friend; if he proves an object of amusement or ridicule, he unwittingly smirks his satisfaction over the effect he is making but fails to observe the glances exchanged in his presence or the silence with which he is greeted—a woman's raising of her lorgnette or a man's irrelevant humming do not serve to abash him.[4]

Case 3

The somewhat pompous head of a large department store was passing through the packing room one day when he saw a boy lounging against a wood box, whistling cheerfully. The boss stopped and looked at him.

[3] Smith, E. D., *Op. cit.*
[4] Dashiell, J. F., *Fundamentals of Objective Psychology.* Houghton Mifflin Co.

"How much do you get a week?" he barked.

"Fifteen dollars."

"Then here's a week's pay—get out."

When the boy was gone, the boss turned to one of his subordinates.

"When did we hire that boy?" he demanded.

"We never hired him," came the astonished answer. "He just brought in a package from another firm."

Problem II

Explain and illustrate from your own observation some causes of misjudgments or false perceptions. State briefly how you think each of these might be remedied.

Case 1

1. One alien saboteur may lead to condemnation of all foreigners.

2. "Don't send any more city boys to work for me!" exclaimed a farmer. "I have just tried one and he didn't even know how to harness a horse. They're all dumbbells on a farm."

Case 2

The girl at the switchboard thinks of the mannequin and how much easier it is just to wear pretty dresses than it is to be a telephone operator. The truck driver thinks how easy it is to do the work of the clerk—simply sitting at a desk. The porter thinks how much easier must be the life of the manager, since he has only to sit at a desk with flowers on it and give orders. The waitress in the restaurant thinks it is easy for the conductor to choose what the orchestra will play and wave his baton while they play it. The window cleaner thinks it must be easy to be the buyer for a department—merely to look at the samples brought in and to buy some of these and some of those.

Case 3

Bill is an experienced office worker who is somewhat morbidly inclined. He is a good, conscientious worker who takes great pride in the accuracy and completeness of his work. This is generally recognized and appreciated by his employer. However, when Bill is asked or told to do anything by his immediate superior, he feels that he is being "bawled out." He has reached the point where he *expects* to be "bawled out" and has developed a chronic "they-don't-appreciate-anything-around-here" complex.

CASE 4

Burnham reports an experiment in which a teacher had her pupils write down the names of five children among their playmates whom they liked best and from these lists ranked the group from the best liked to the least popular. The children were given no idea of the purpose of this, and they soon forgot about it. Later the teacher placed the five best liked and the five least popular in a row in front of the room, alternating the ones most liked with those least popular. Then she said to the other children in the room:

"I am going to give the children who are placed here a short exercise in gymnastics. You must give accurate attention."

Then she gave the command, "Attention! Right arm high. Arm down." In accordance with secret instructions, the children liked best raised their left, instead of their right, arms, and only the children not liked gave the correct response.

Immediately after the exercise, the teacher asked the class to write down the names of those who had raised their right hands correctly and those who had made errors. To those children well liked, not one of whom had carried out the exercise correctly, a higher percentage of correct performance was always ascribed than to those not liked. All possibilities that the children purposely favored those they liked at the expense of those they did not like were excluded by the teacher, and further experiments justified this assumption.[5]

CASE 5

Even small and transient bodily disturbances temporarily may upset the mind. If we eat something that disagrees with digestion, we may find the whole day ruined. We may become curt, snappy, irritable, and difficult. Our judgments are poor and hasty; we are unfair and inconsistent.[6]

[5] Burnham, W. H., *The Wholesome Personality*. D. Appleton-Century Co., Inc.

[6] Strecker, E. A., and Appel, K. F., *Discovering Ourselves*. The Macmillan Co.

UNIT VI

Emotional Behavior

Objectives

1. *To recognize the functions of emotion in human behavior: (a) to know how emotions arise, (b) to understand the conflict with social controls.*
2. *To realize that differences in emotionality are due to: (a) physiological differences, and (b) past or present environmental differences.*
3. *To develop a program of prevention and redirection of harmful emotions.*
4. *To appreciate that emotional control contributes to emotional maturity.*

INTRODUCTION

When people are considering their own or other people's behavior, the meaning of the word *emotion* is quite clear for practical purposes without the need of a technical definition. Anyone will remember from personal experience what it feels like to be angry, joyful, tender, afraid, anxious, etc. All these states of human consciousness have one thing in common, namely, a heightened feeling that may be termed *tension*. One feels a state of tension within himself, and he has a strong urge to do something to discharge that tension. The wisdom of the language expresses this idea in such popular phrases as "bursting with excitement"; "could not contain himself for joy"; "boiling with rage"; "torn by anxiety."

The built-up tension must be discharged in some way. The rate of its discharge and the pathways that the discharge follows are of great importance to the workings of the human

73

body. It is important for the student of human relations to realize that the emotional state is more than a mere "state of mind." Under emotional tension, neither the mind nor the muscle is free; there is fumbling in thinking and acting. Most people, from personal experience, are familiar with the confusion and clumsiness that often result from embarrassment. Under states of tension, the internal organs may also fumble. Feelings of dryness in the mouth and throat are due to altered functions of the salivary glands. The feeling of having a lump in the throat, sudden loss of appetite, a weight in the pit of the stomach, or, sometimes, even diarrhea, all may indicate the effects of emotional tensions upon internal organs.

MILD EMOTIONS

In the main, this unit is aimed at the causes and effects of violent emotions such as anger, fear, and shock. However, in order that attention be not centered exclusively upon the harmful effects of the stronger emotions, certain facts should be noted regarding the milder ones.

1. The mild emotions are tonic to the physical system. That this effect is commonly recognized is to be observed in the encouragement of pleasant conversation at mealtimes, and in the use of games, singing, and competition in social groups. Teachers, supervisors, parents, and other leaders are trained in the art of control by pleasant incentives. Poffenberger once declared in a class lecture that people in general would be physically better if doing more work with the stimulating effect of reasonable incentives than they would be if doing far less work with the humdrum of boredom or antagonism.

2. Prescott emphasizes the fact that these mild emotions do not necessarily have to be pleasing in order to produce this tonic effect. It takes only common sense to recognize that the clear, fair correction, the specific showing of consequences of poor work or bad attitudes, or even the timely "spanking" may have their wholesome effects. Again, a challenge can often be the making of a man. (Unfortunately this last idea is recog-

nized and appropriated by certain "drivers" of the old school as an alibi for their negative and temperamental moods.)

3. Any of the milder emotions may shift suddenly into violent ones. —Who has not seen a game end in a fight? In such a case, the bodily mechanisms that provided increased energy for the pleasantly stimulating game now furnish still greater energy for the violence of the fight. The same thing happens when wholesome caution turns to fear or panic, or when bracing spirit turns to rage.

BODILY EFFECTS OF STRONG EMOTIONS

H. Goldberg (*Philadelphia Ledger*) says of these changes: "The emergency calls forth carbohydrates stored in the liver, which results in flooding the blood with sugar for increased energy; blood is taken away from the digestive system and distributed in greater quantities to the heart for greater effort, to the lungs for more oxygen, to the central nervous system and the limbs. Thus the body is ready for fight, flight, or struggle of some kind." The same writer compares the management of a body thus prepared for action, but subjected to the rigid controls necessary in modern social conditions, to the driving of an automobile with one foot on the gas and the other on the brake. How often can people in modern society afford either to fight or to run from their enemies? If the body is charged with surplus glandular materials for increased muscular strength that cannot be used, adjustment becomes confusion.

Before going further with this discussion of bodily changes, it will be worthwhile to recall briefly the muscles and glands which in Unit II were cited as the *reactors* in bodily activity.

There are two general classes of muscles in the body. We shall find that they are both affected by emotions. First there are the striped, or voluntary, muscles, which respond to the will of the individual. These are found in the arms, the legs, and, in fact, in any part of the body where movement is controlled at will. We depend upon the striped muscles to accomplish any overt act. Most of us have observed or experienced times during which sheer muscular strength far surpassed what could normally be expected. Those likely were times of emotional stress. Then there is the intricate system of smooth, or involuntary, muscles, which constitute the moving parts of the various internal organs. In swallowing, for instance, one begins by voluntary movements that may easily turn into choking under emotional tension. The subsequent peristaltic action of the esophagus (smooth-muscular action) can become so upset as to stop, or even reverse, and one regurgitates what was being dispatched downward.

The stomach is very active during normal digestion, churning the food about vigorously. This action is accomplished by several layers of smooth muscle. When the food-mass has reached a certain chemical and physical state, the smooth muscles that constrict the outlet from the stomach into the small intestine relax, and the food passes through. All these muscles, and those at other points along the intestinal tract, are greatly influenced by emotional tension. It is at these points of possible stricture under violent emotional states that so much damage is done to the health of high-tempered or excitable people. Other systems, such as the heart, blood vessels, and the smaller air passages of the lungs, are, like the digestive system, under the influence of emotion. We recall from the discussion of the endocrine glands in Unit II that, under the influence of emotion, the adrenal glands secrete varying amounts of the hormone adrenalin. Now adrenalin, in significant quantities, of course, tends to increase the fighting or muscular power of the body. It stimulates the rate of the heartbeat, raises the blood pressure, mobilizes a lot of glycogen which will be used as fuel by the muscles, opens air passages of the lungs, etc.

Such elaborate internal preparations are no doubt very valuable to the lower animals, or were so even to primitive men, in meeting the demands made upon them either by danger or by unusual efforts necessary to satisfy their wants. They are even valuable for the occasional true emergency in modern life. However, under conditions of present civilization, this tuning up for tremendous effort cannot often be followed by direct action, which would give opportunity for a full and direct discharge. The result is that the individual who experiences this emotional crisis is left very much in a state like that accompanying an uncompleted sneeze, only worse. The tension that has been created, if it does not find its normal outlet, discharges inwardly, playing havoc with internal processes.

AUTONOMIC NERVOUS SYSTEM

In Unit II of this book, brief consideration was given to the *central* and the *peripheral* parts of the human nervous system. In order not to complicate the picture of stimulus-response activity, which it was then necessary to discuss, no mention was made of the third part—the *autonomic* nervous system. It now is necessary to look at that third part because it is the key to the series of bodily changes involved in emotional behavior.

The word *autonomic* comes from two Greek roots meaning "self-ruling," and it was applied to this part of the nervous system because it was once thought to be independent of the central and peripheral systems. The name is still applicable if we think of the autonomic system as controlling an intricate variety of inner workings of the body without our having to give any thought to them. However, the impulses that traverse the autonomic still have to come from several parts of the brain, and they must come via the spinal cord.

The autonomic system, sketched roughly in Figure 3, is arranged in two opposing divisions—the *sympathetic* in the center, and the *parasympathetic* above and below the other. In Figure 3, the sympathetic nerve lines are represented by broken lines and the parasympathetic, by solid lines. Study of the sketch will disclose that each of the organs and glands in the column at the right is reached by *both* the broken lines of the sympathetic and the solid lines of the parasympathetic. (The sketch is simplified and does not show a complete listing of organs and glands so affected.)

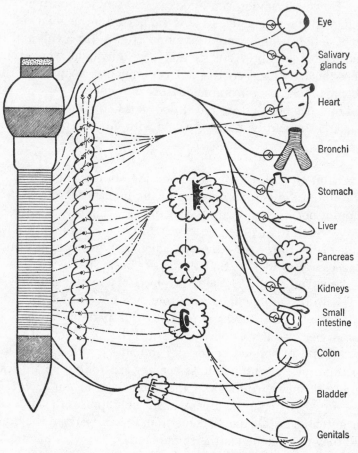

Fig. 3. General Structure and Organization of the Autonomic Nervous System.

The *sympathetic* is so named because it acts in "sympathy" with the pleasantness or unpleasantness of our perceptions. Any particular situation may anger, amuse, scare, or interest an individual according to his understanding or interpretation of that situation or event. The meaning of the stimulus-situation to an individual, or his confidence in his ability to deal with it, determine whether or not that situation arouses his emotions. Once the individual has arrived at his perception, impulses passing through the *sympathetic* have the right-of-way under fear, anger, exultation, or any violent emotion, and they prepare the body for vigorous action. This preparation for quick effort includes processes previously referred to, such as slowing up digestion, speeding circulation, and releasing energizing secretions. The endocrines are intimately related to this system. They influence it and are influenced by it. The adrenal gland, for instance, secretes adrenalin when it is stimulated by the sympathetic nervous system, but adrenalin has a peculiar way of stimulating in turn the sympathetic system, so that these two reactions reinforce each other. The ultimate purpose of the *sympathetic* is to serve as a sudden mobilizer of bodily energy for fight, flight, or struggle.

The word "parasympathetic" means "beside the sympathetic," but mere juxtaposition is the only excuse for the name; the function of the *parasympathetic* is to achieve the exact opposite of the *sympathetic*. Demobilization is as important as mobilization after the crisis has been met. Like the sympathetic, the parasympathetic also depends upon our *perceptions* for the "green light" on the calming-down process. If an individual perceives a disturbance as having been eliminated, then the emotion disappears, and the *parasympathetic* is free to bring the body back to normal. Even during an emergency, this balancing influence may be present in an individual conditioned to "keep" his head, or act with poise.

PREVENTION AND REDIRECTION

Understanding and redirection of these emotional disturbances are clearly vital for the individual in his maintenance of his own health, in his interpretation of the moods of superiors, and in his attempts to deal wisely and constructively with subordinates or other associates. It cannot be denied, of course, that individuals in the human race differ as to glandular, smooth-muscular, and nervous make-up and must therefore differ somewhat in emotionality. However, the major portion of human emotionality is due to attitudes, which, of course, are only learned habits that can be changed or replaced. Bearing in mind the physiological disturbances that have been outlined in this discussion and in the cases to follow, one is apt to recognize the wisdom of the old adage: "An ounce of prevention is worth a pound of cure." In fact, this maxim supplies the names for the two parts of a program for redirection of emotionality.

Preventive. Little time is required to argue the point that if one does not get disturbed in the first place, he avoids the process of having to recover from the disturbance. Here again the equation $A + I = P$ is useful. Since emotional disturbance results from our perceptions, if we did not perceive things emotionally, we would not necessarily become emotionally disturbed. For perception is a result of our interpretation, and hence everything depends upon how we interpret a stimulus situation. Therefore, an obvious rule would be: *Interpret situations in such a way as not to become emotionally disturbed.* This, of course, is easier to state than do. However, any person who is interested in his personal effectiveness, to say nothing of his health, will reflect at length on the above rule. It requires the altering of some attitudes; for instance, one must refine his juvenile and frantic defense of the ego. As Gates says, "Emotions we recognize as subjective, as due to conditions in us." [1] Every time that we can successfully prevent the sympathetic nervous system from getting us internally wrought up, we have taken one more step toward emotional maturity.

Curative. If we have failed at the preventive level—and who is so perfect as never to slip?—then we must look to the cure. The influences needed to bring the *parasympathetic* into operation are *substitute activities.* The Army recognizes this principle. The infantryman is trained in a whole series of quick, purposefully planned, *thought-diverting activities.* "Hitting the dirt," throwing off the rifle safety catch, and camouflaging

[1] Gates, A. I., *Elementary Psychology.* The Macmillan Co.

his position are activities that tend to divert attention from the dangers that might disturb the soldier.

Since the "spotlight of attention" can be on only one idea at any given instant, if it is occupied with specific, directed activities, it cannot then be building emotional perceptions. In cases of air raids, fires, or floods, persons serving on active committees with given duties are known to be those least stirred by fears. So, in the case of the person who has already become emotionally disturbed, another obvious rule would be: *Divert the "spotlight" of attention from the disturbing concept and focus it upon something else.*

If the "something else" is some physical activity, so much the better, for then there is an avenue of discharge of tension. The man who has developed a variety of interests is fortunate in that he has a choice of several outlets and can find release in one sphere when blocked in another. Sports, crafts, the arts —these are pathways of discharge of the greatest value. Their cultivation by every human being is as analogously important as lightning rods on barns or safety valves on steam boilers.

The brain is the control-center, the real seat of authority in man. If ignorance, superstition, or unsound attitudes rule the mind, then good digestion, normal blood pressure, or wholesome glandular action cannot be expected. On the other hand, intelligent habits of "second thought," better understanding of situations and how to handle them, or prompt diverting of attention through intelligent activity will shift the flow of nerve impulses from the sympathetic into the more constructive channels of the parasympathetic.

(*Note:* A satisfactory definition of *emotion* is an extremely difficult thing to find. Discussion groups might gain some benefit in evaluating the following one from James W. Wilson:[2] "An emotion is an affective state of consciousness which is dependent upon the interpretation of a stimulus situation and results in a mobilization of energy.")

[2] Director of educational research at the Rochester Institute of Technology, in psychology lecture notes.

Problem I

How may a manager of employees benefit by understanding the nature of the physical effects of the mild emotions?

CASE 1

Some natural causes are being discovered in the study of the glands for many human reactions commonly attributed to laziness, faking, or state of mind. An individual is tired at, say, ten o'clock; half an hour later he is feeling fine. He has not stopped to rest, nor has he taken food. Good news, a break in the clouds indicating fair weather, recognition of work well done—any of these or similar intangibles may help to restore bodily energy and serve purposes equivalent to those served by rest or sleep.

CASE 2

To the average person the language of physiology may sound strange and difficult, but for centuries natural leaders have been applying the principles of physical stimulation through encouragement, although they may not have understood them.

1. Napoleon, pointing to the great pyramids on his Egyptian campaign, said to his soldiers, "Forty centuries look down upon you."

2. The father of a leg-weary child cut a stick horse for him and told him to ride. The child raced home with no further thought of his fatigued leg muscles.

3. Bill's job seems to be to watch for "choke-points" in the production line. When work begins to pile up at such a point, Bill appears on the scene with an enthusiastic "Let's go!" and begins. The renewed efforts of the regular men at the point make it unnecessary for Bill to stay long.

4. The exhausted sportsman carrying his boat across a portage is on the point of giving up. But from the top of a hill he discovers that the lake is a mile or more ahead of him; then he walks briskly on and puts the boat into the water.

Problem II
How may emotional disturbances affect health?

CASE 1

If a cat which has been fed a meal of gruel containing bismuth, a substance opaque to X-rays, is placed before the screen of a fluoroscope, the normal rhythmic, churning movements of the stomach may be clearly observed. If the cat is angered by a barking dog, these movements may be greatly diminished; in fact, they often cease altogether. The glandular activities of digestion are similarly diminished. In a typical experiment on an angered dog, instead of the usual sixty-five or seventy cubic centimeters of gastric juice the amount secreted was less than nine cubic centimeters (and this of poor quality). Thus the whole digestive process is side-tracked.[3]

CASE 2

In a recent study conducted at the Massachusetts General Hospital it was found that a large proportion of patients suffering from asthma, arthritis, and inflammation of the intestines were victims of chronic emotional tension. Personal interviews revealed that 96 per cent of the last named group were harboring resentments—some against employers, some against teachers, and others against parents.[4]

CASE 3

An employee has been publicly reprimanded by his foreman. His anger flares up, but he dares not reply. He is afraid of losing his job. Hence, he represses the strong fear-rage emotion, and it remains stored up within him. That night he may snap back at his wife, or angrily send his children to bed for some minor misdemeanor. If the trouble with his foreman goes on for days and weeks, and he must still repress his anger-fear emotion, he may become literally unbearable at home. His digestion may go wrong, which will make him still less bearable. Fright about himself may now be added to his anger at his foreman. This again will increase his digestive disorder. And so the unhappy process may continue.[5]

[3] Gates, A. I., *Op. cit.*
[4] Gray, G. W., "Anxiety and Illness." *Harper's Magazine* (reprinted in *Reader's Digest*, June, 1939).
[5] Overstreet, H. A., *About Ourselves: Psychology for Normal People.* W. W. Norton & Co.

Problem III

How did man develop emotional tendencies that handicap him under modern social arrangements?

CASE 1

The rabbit is sitting quietly on his haunches in the warm spring sun, a long way from his burrow. Suddenly, just across the clearing, he hears a crackling in the bushes. Perhaps he senses a doggy smell. Long before he sees anything, a toning-up for effort has taken place within him—a mechanical reaction, inherited from endless ages of rabbits and developed in himself since he was a little rabbit and heard his mother tell what dogs had done to his furry father. And the moment the sense of danger comes, the suprarenals begin to act. His lungs expand, he breathes quickly, deeply; his blood pressure goes up, his heart begins to beat rapidly, all his muscles are tense. His whole rabbit organism has been thrown into "high gear" —what for? Why had nature, down through countless rabbit ages, developed these reactions? So the rabbit might get a start on the oncoming dog, run back to his burrow, and save his life. For him, all these fear emotions are *protective reactions*. They have some meaning; some sense; some use. He reacts to them. Off he goes, and the extra strength and tension of muscle and nerve—called up by the adrenalin—gets him back to his burrow in safety. Here he rests—his blood pressure goes down, his heart stops working over-time, his breathing becomes regular, and, unless the dog is pawing still at the mouth of the burrow, his suprarenals stop working and the adrenalin that had been poured into his blood is used up in the process of his flight and disappears.

But how different the whole thing becomes when you consider the same process in a human being! . . . Perhaps in the future when men are better trained in such things, when they get a fright they will go to someone whom they know and trust, will tell him what has happened, and say, "I am simply scared almost to death, come on out and let's have a round of golf." But nowadays, most men keep their mouths shut. They can't run away; there's nothing to run away from—nothing material like the rabbit's pursuing dog. So they sit and stew in their own fear.[6]

[6] Oliver, J. R., *Fear*. New York: The Macmillan Co.

Case 2

In a small city there lives today an elderly man who is gifted by nature with a pleasing personality and an excellent tenor voice. He is well known to all the grocers of the city and can get a salesman's position when he so desires. But he holds each job only a few weeks. Quick to take offense, he is not on a job very long until he finds annoyances too great for him to endure, and he quits. His singing is in demand, but he lasts only a few weeks at a time in any church choir. He lives with his family in a house and in a section far inferior to many who have far less ability and none of his special talents.

Case 3

Further light upon "The Emergency Theory of the Emotions" and its bearing upon man's present problem of understanding the situation is given by Overstreet: "Let us suppose that a person is faced with a situation causing rage or fear. The adrenal glands are stimulated to the heightened activity. Adrenal secretion is introduced into the blood stream. As a result, the blood is withdrawn from the cranial and intestinal regions and pumped into the running and fighting muscles. The organism is put into a condition either to fight or to escape. If, now, the individual does fight or does use his legs to run away, the glandular secretion is consumed in the muscular processes. But if there are no muscular processes, if the raging creature must stand mute and unresisting before his tormentor, or the frightened creature must move no limb, it is exactly like taking food into the stomach and being unable to digest it." [7]

Problem IV

How may one develop healthful emotional prevention or control?

Case 1

A few years ago a young man of exceptional talents left his pioneer farm environment and entered the preparatory department of a state university. With the first break of spring he began to be restless and dissatisfied. He mistook his emotions for evidence that he was "not built for confinement." Accordingly, he went

[7] Overstreet, H. A., *Op. cit.*

into a railroad construction camp as a laborer. There the work soon became monotonous, and his restlessness returned. His next jump was to a teacher training school, where he soon got a certificate. But again, restlessness grew worse than ever. The years of youth were swiftly passing. After a time, he settled down on a homestead with the feeling that somehow he had failed. A younger brother saw in this experience the application of the old saying, "A bird never flies so far but his tail follows him."

CASE 2

Many of the most active workers of the world have owed their ability to stand up under exacting schedules to habits of taking short periods of absolute rest. How can one remove worries, special interests, or excitement from his mind? The radio is proving an up-to-date substitute for "counting sheep," tracing patterns on wallpaper, or thinking of tired muscles. Certain individuals with long work hours and much to worry about have more or less accidentally hit upon the device of turning on the radio, lying down, and listening until they fall asleep, waking in a few minutes "as good as new."

CASE 3

Hate amounts to little more than extended and repeated anger perceptions. Worry is little more than extended and repeated fear perceptions.

Does the discussion in the first part of this unit offer any explanation of why man is told not to bear grudges or worry?

Does the preventive-curative program of emotional re-education offer any suggestions as to how to avoid hating and worrying?

UNIT VII

Problem Solving

Objectives

1. *To identify the methods of approaching problems.*
2. *To recognize the adjustment mechanisms that people use for self-justification or other satisfaction.*
3. *To practice the greater tolerance that comes with understanding the functions of the mechanisms.*
4. *To develop more effective habits in solving problems.*

INTRODUCTION

Practically any waking moment of a person's life may present a problem. To go further, nearly all of living is problem solving. Thinking as psychologists, let us consider the person as a psyche, or an ego, or, better yet, as a personality. The personality is constantly meeting situations of one sort or another, great or small. The personality feels that its body is hungry, or that it wants to laugh, or that its scalp itches, or that it wants to murder its grandmother, or that it should get married, or that it wants a drink of water, etc.

What happens when the personality is confronted with a situation? First, there is a period of attempted adjustment. Here the personality tries to adjust the situation to its liking or itself to the situation. The period of adjustment may be short if the problem is simple, or if the situation is so common that the personality has already established habitual ways of handling it. For instance, it does not take long to adjust to a little itch of the scalp, unless, of course, the individual is in some unusual circumstance, such as being confined in a strait jacket or playing the role of a corpse before an audience. On the other hand, a more involved problem, one less habitual, such as deciding what college to attend or whether to apply for an out-of-town job, might require a considerably longer period.

The result of this period must be either adjustment or maladjustment. In the case of adjustment the problem is solved, at least for the moment. If maladjustment, a whole new set of problems is presented. The boy wants the car, but funds are not at hand; the sportsman looks longingly at the trophy, but the necessary training is a long and uphill pull; the fox craves the grapes, but they are in the top of the vine, the supervisor is concerned about his production schedules, but his workers are uninterested, untrained, or poorly equipped.

FOUR APPROACHES TO PROBLEMS

Face to face with a problem, the individual has four ways in which he may seek adjustment:

1. He may attack his problem directly.

Remember the *Job Relations Training* formula quoted in Unit V: get the facts; weigh and decide; take action; follow up.

2. He may discover by sound reasoning that the particular aim he has in mind is not attainable, and, by equally sound reasoning, select another worthy and more attainable objective.

3. He may quit, that is, abandon his objective and walk out.

One who blinds himself to obligation, or accepts no challenge, may feel some relief by "forgetting" his responsibilities.

4. He may try to bypass his problem, at least temporarily, through the use of some adjustment mechanism.

In man's Western civilization there have grown up more or less commonly accepted attitudes toward the first three of these approaches. The direct attack is considered noble and praiseworthy; there is no denying that it gets things done. The substitute goal is accepted as reasonable and constructive, and, on occasion, may partake of some of the glamour of the first. The quitter is looked upon with contempt, and, in spite of his philosophizing to the contrary, he usually suffers some degree of self-depreciation. Understanding of the fourth approach is not so common as that of the other three, and, even though all people employ the adjustment mechanisms, there have not grown up such well-defined mass attitudes regarding their use. It is the aim of this unit to promote some better understanding of the adjustment mechanisms.

Adjustment Mechanisms

Just as a physical mechanism is a device with which to accomplish some material job, so a psychological mechanism is a mental device to accomplish some less tangible task. Such mechanisms have been called *escape* or *defense* mechanisms because they represent an attempt to escape the rough treatment of reality or to defend the ego against blame. *Adjustment* is the term used in this unit because the mechanisms are used in a period of attempted adjustment, and because there is some question as to whether they may *always* be said to arise from defense or escape motives.

The following is a list of terms applied by psychologists to some of the more common impulsive, or emotional, mechanisms for dealing with blockings, interferences, or disappointments.

Rationalization (Self-justification). "When an ardent desire makes that which is unsound appear rational and thereby brings about self-indulgence through self-deception," says Elliott Dunlap Smith, "the process is called 'rationalization.' . . . Instances of rationalization are legion. We rationalize before an act in order to persuade ourselves that it is right to do it, and after the act in order to spare ourselves the pain of admitting that we have done wrong. . . . Revenge often passes censorship as justice or discipline. Slander or abuse successfully passes censorship by the use of such passwords as 'to be frank with you,' 'it wouldn't be honest not to say,' or 'calling a spade a spade.'" [1]

Wish-thinking. If a person kids himself into believing that

[1] Smith, E. D., *Op. cit.*

what he *wishes* to be true *is* true, he is guilty of wish-thinking. Overstreet says, "The strong emotion is a wish." After giving numerous examples of wish-thinking, he concludes: "The advance of civilization has meant the gradual extension of the area of fact-thinking. The invention of the tool was the initial triumph of such thinking. A tool cannot be wished or prayed into existence. The toolmaker had to grapple with the tough conditions of reality. He had to meet them with honesty and efficiency. He could neither evade them nor fabricate them. It is for this reason that toolmaking all through the ages— the moulding of matter in usable shape—has been one of the most effective means whereby man has disciplined himself into straight and honest thinking." [2]

Negative compensation (bluffing). Whether or not a person suffers any real lack in his make-up, if he *perceives* himself as inferior, he may indulge in some form of compensation. In *negative* compensation, the individual, being more or less aware of a certain weakness, seeks to "cover up" by affecting signs of strength in the particular trait in which he is weak. Just as a cat's fur stands on end in order to appear larger when he faces a dog, so a person, more or less unconsciously sensing personal ineffectiveness, may use loud and threatening language or gestures to make himself seem more powerful than he really is. These tricks of negative compensation are now becoming so widely understood that it is becoming more and more difficult to make such bluffing effective.

Constructive compensation (sublimation). Compensation may have its positive as well as its negative forms. Intelligent or intuitive substitutions of other goals for goals unavoidably cut off, or the development of certain personality attributes to make up for other unavoidable shortcomings, have accounted for many of the world's greatest achievements. In cases of severe reverses in his pursuit of satisfaction in one field of thought or action, the individual often throws his fullest energies into another line of effort and, by so doing, is able to

[2] Overstreet, H. A., *Op. cit.*

forget or lose sight of his losses through his greater accomplishments in the second field.

Submission or compromise. Like all other ways of escape from dissatisfaction, *submission* has both its beneficial and its negative sides. Negatively, it is akin to surrender or retreat. To give in too rapidly to someone's else ideas may brand an individual as a "yes man." On the other hand, it is most effective to realize when it is best to concede a point, to accept the other fellow's point of view, or even to "lie low"—that has in it the substance of co-operation. Moreover, in either phase, submission gives release from emotional conflict. Whether it be called retreat or intelligent compromise or co-operation depends upon the occasion. Even military history shows that there is a time to retreat or defend, as well as a time to attack.

Projection. When annoyed by inability to succeed at some endeavor, the individual may soothe his injured pride by blaming someone else or some condition in the environment for his own failure. On the Day of Atonement, the ancient Hebrews would choose a goat by lot, confess their sins over it, and turn it loose in the wilderness to take their guilt away with it. In later eras, a young prince would take a boy with him to school to take his punishments for him. Scapegoating is well known today. Our modern scapegoats, or whipping boys, are often people or minority groups more defenseless than ourselves.

Prejudice. By closing his mind to realities unfavorable to his immediate desires, the individual saves himself the discomfort of admitting there is any good in whatever stands in his way; or, he may escape the discomfort of admitting that there is anything wrong with his pet projects or his personal favorites. This is sometimes called "the logic-tight compartment of the mind."

Sour grapes. Instead of working harder to secure a desired object, the individual may ease his conscience by declaring that the object is of little value anyway. It tends to soothe the man who lost his job to dwell on the way in which the work was injuring his health. The jilted lover may quote, "A woman is only a woman, but a good cigar is a smoke!"

Sweet lemon (pollyanna). The happy faculty of reading some reward into every situation, no matter how disappointing, supplies to many people an escape from admitting failure. Instead of being sad over the car shortage, one may enjoy the money he is saving or his freedom from responsibility.

Daydreams. These flights of imagination, which furnish all mankind with so much low-priced entertainment, can be divided into three subclasses:

Conquering hero dreams. Being unable to deliver the grand oration, make the football team, or possess the streamlined car, the individual may realize satisfaction by imagining himself swaying a great audience, carrying the ball in the Rose Bowl for the winning touchdown that is broadcast throughout the nation, or being a part of the grand parade in his gorgeously decorated automobile.

Suffering hero dreams. Denied sympathy or appreciation in real life, one may in imagination pay the price of suffering and death in order to see himself as the noble martyr who has earned the adulation of mankind.

Regressive dreams. If heating the bottle and changing the baby's underthings is not very inspiring, the young father can dream of the nights when he borrowed dad's car and went out with the gang. The girl who is losing out in her love-life will find no such problems in playing with her dolls. There is always some pleasant era of the past to which to flee.

Nomadism. The person who can always persuade himself that to skip to a new job or a new location means a chance to better himself is spared having to work out satisfactory solutions of the old problems.

Hysteria. In direct surrender there is often real emotional release from struggle. Individuals have been known to go to bed, throw themselves upon charity, or even take their own lives rather than fight on against great odds. Usually, however, hysteria refers to more strictly physical ailments brought on by intense emotional conflict. *Psychology for the Fighting Man,* published by the National Research Council, treats this subject vividly and interestingly, as it does many other topics of interest to those supervising people in any kind of modern situation. It is from this book that the following three paragraphs are adapted:

When disappointment or strain becomes too great for the soldier to stand up under, he may literally "go over the hill," or may pretend illness. However, he may actually become ill and be honestly unaware of the connection between his sudden sickness and the disturbing situation confronting him. Such mentally caused illnesses are real enough, even though they have no organic basis. And it is in the most conscientious persons—those who try most earnestly to succeed—that they usually occur. Hysterical blindness, deafness, or paralysis, and the war neurosis miscalled "shell shock" in World War I have this sort of origin.

When the soldier reaches the point where he can stand up no longer under the horrors he must face, when he can walk no farther and can fight no more, and yet his spirit will not allow him to turn back, then he may go blind, or lose the use of his arms or legs, or forget his name and everything connected with his identity. Major Frederick Hanson of Montreal, in discussing such cases of exhaustion, is reported to have said that some soldiers were treated in base hospitals, and that many of these were able to return to the front. But with those who were given rest and medical care right at the front, within sound of the guns, a far greater percentage of recovery was realized.

Each man, no matter how strong mentally and physically, has his limits beyond which the strongest will cannot drive him. Unless he learns his own tolerances and acts accordingly, *nature* may have to provide these *peculiar forms of escape* from pain or emotion that is too intense to be endured.

MECHANISMS ARE NORMAL

In thinking over the aforementioned mechanisms, the student should fix clearly in mind certain facts involved. In the first place, the individual daydreaming his troubles away, or harboring delusions of persecution, or seeing only his side of the argument is not clearly conscious of his own self-deception. He is tricked into unsound reasoning by his own feelings. Studies prove that the most conscientious of drivers, when involved in a collision, tend to see the other fellows' mistakes much more clearly than they do their own.

Another important point is that these deceptions, for which emotions are responsible, are common experiences of normal, successful people. In fact, the emotional background from which they arise may possibly even indicate superiority. ". . . the lower down the animal scale one goes the less guilt sense there is, while the higher up one goes the more it is apparent. A dog may be made to feel guilty, probably not a cat, and certainly not a chicken, or a species still more rudimentary in brain structure." [3] It is true that the "Napoleonic" delusion and other fixed complexes are characteristic, and even most conspicuous, in certain types of serious illness. These phases of abnormal psychology are interesting; however, attention is here directed not to the extremes of emotional reactions, with their deplorable effects on weaker natures, but rather to the tricks that feelings play on so-called "normal" people.

Cases to follow suggest how easy it is for feelings or emotions to switch the mind from straight, to wishful, thinking. When the going is difficult, the temptation to avoid the issue is strong. The important points to bear in mind in studying these well-known types of emotional reaction are that they are natural human tendencies, that they are not necessarily wholly bad, and that it is no sign of abnormality in an individual if he finds that he has been practicing some or all of them. Probably

[3] Bisch, L. E., *Be Glad You're Neurotic.* New York: McGraw-Hill Book Co., Inc.

no man or woman of worth or imagination has not indulged in building air castles, in enjoying sour grapes, or even in buck passing. It is only when these emotional tricks become *substitutes for real effort* or when they result in misjudgment of others that they become a danger.

In the more extreme cases, when fatigue or other cause of lack of endurance is present, emotional conflict may lead to both mental and physical breakdown. The fact that the foregoing discussion of hysteria was based on experience in the battlefield does not mean that it is confined to war alone. Amnesia, for example, has been called "the shell shock of civil life." Violent emotional stresses and strains are by no means confined to the battlefield. If we are to be able to understand ourselves and others, we must consider this phase of human nature and experience.

Straight thinking. Whether one is the stronger type of personality, in danger only of being trapped into unsound judgments, or whether he is the type who is in danger of physical or mental breakdown, the remedy is in substance the same. He must build his own reservoirs of power through:

1. The plain processes of intelligent habit formation.
2. The application of the established principles of learning.
3. The facing of facts.
4. The scientific attitude of problem approach used in practically all other units in this course.

Through persistent, intelligent practice, the average man may build *habits* of straight thinking.

Problem I

In the following case situations, identify the approach to the problem and types of mechanisms.

CASE 1

Joe was convinced that his foreman did not like him. Jobs given to Joe seemed the hardest and dirtiest in the department. His foreman was gruff and difficult to approach. Joe's first resolve was to quit. Later, he decided to try whether he could not either change the man's attitude or know why not. Someone in the department told Joe that the foreman was a racing fan. The next morning, Joe clipped the entry lists, checked his choices of winners, and asked the foreman's opinion. They had a free and friendly talk about the horses. Soon they were much better acquainted, and Joe's situation became very satisfactory.

Case 2

A factory foreman found that one of his young employees had become slow, sullen, and disinterested in his work. The foreman did nothing for a few weeks because he assumed that the employee had a sound reason for his change of conduct. Finally, he determined to discharge him. On second thought, he decided to ask one of the young man's friends for any information that might explain his behavior, and learned that his father had recently been sentenced to a long term in prison. The foreman realized that the man was wasting his energy in feeling sorry for himself and in hating the world, and arranged a half hour of uninterrupted conversation with him. By using a friendly tone and manner with the employee, the foreman was able to show the young man that his present difficulty was an opportunity for him to prove to the world that most of the members of his family were honest and useful citizens. He was able to convince the employee that if he wished to do so, either he might become a drifter and eventually develop into another social outcast or he might use the situation as a challenge for the future.[4]

Case 3

Nothing is so likely to change the young industrial radical into a conservative as the task of hiring some of the industrial misfits, supervising their work, and then meeting their payroll.

Case 4

Very plain women often are noted for pleasing dispositions.

Case 5

G. displayed a marked bravado and cocksureness, caring nothing for the opinions of others; and he was blunt to the extent of ill manners in his criticism of both textbook and teacher. Though all

[4] Hepner, H. W., *Human Relations in Changing Industry*. New York: Prentice-Hall, Inc.

respected his ability, he had no friends among his classmates. It is hard to believe that the origin of these traits was extreme shyness and sensitiveness. Yet such was the case. As a child he could not bear to be laughed at, and his very sensitiveness and self-consciousness made him the object of playful ridicule among his playmates and elders. The result was that he withdrew within himself, and gradually built up a defensory wall of social behavior. Society was at first his tormentor and enemy. Then he developed a superior indifference to it, and took every occasion to show this attitude in his outspoken criticisms and eccentric ways. At college, his life was that of an unpopular recluse. If his nature was bitter, however, it was strong. His self-recognized compensation for unpopularity was academic standing. He worked assiduously and obtained high grades so that he "could cram down the world's throat that the poor stick whom nobody likes can get high marks if he cares to take the trouble." [5]

CASE 6

The "buck-passer" is a familiar figure in state, industry, home, and school:

The employment office sends out such poor material.

The economic system offers no opportunity for success.

The poor housekeeper could do so much "if she had anything to do it with."

The student fails because the examination is made of "catch questions."

The teacher makes such a poor showing because her students are lazy.

CASE 7

There is the "conquering hero" type of dream, in which the individual catches a forward pass and runs for the winning touchdown. Of such is the stuff of fairy tales with the poor little girl coming into glory in the last scene of the drama. The conquering hero, under the influence of his reveries, is as intoxicated as the drunkard who, under the influence of alcohol, "can lick any man in the county." [6]

CASE 8

Supervisor X is always the agreeable one in conference. "Yes, Mr. —," is his favorite comment on all policies proposed by his

[5] Allport, F. A., *Social Psychology.* New York: Houghton Mifflin Co.
[6] Vaughan, W. F., *Op. cit.*

superior. Back in his department, he assumes the martyr-like "orders are orders" attitude.

Supervisor Y argues a point as long as he can hold the floor. After a ruling contrary to his own views has been announced, his attitude in his department is, "Don't ask *me*. I did all *I* could to make 'em see the light."

CASE 9

The writer has an acquaintance who obtained a good position as chief clerk in a business office. It was soon apparent that he could not get along with his office force. Actually his failure to control the situation boiled down to two facts, that he did not give adequate directions for what he wanted done, and then when annoyed by an error he shouted at the offender, making a public display of what could have been settled quietly. His subordinates were generally efficient workers, and they resented having the mistakes made through inadequate guidance aired so conspicuously. The man sensed the attitude of hostility readily enough, worried about his failure, and one day he did not come to work. Inquiry revealed that he had left town. He is now living on the family homestead in the country. His defects are not only unremedied, but intensified by the bitterness of failure.[7]

[7] Pressy, S. L., *Psychology and the New Education.* New York: Harper & Brothers.

UNIT VIII

Acting on Suggestion

Objectives

1. *To direct attention to the role suggestion plays in everyday living.*
2. *To recognize the importance of suggestion in influencing others, and in resisting undesirable influences.*
3. *To recognize the need for governing one's own behavior by conscious thought.*
4. *To recognize the basic principles employed by one who wishes to influence the behavior of others.*

INTRODUCTION

Acting on suggestion is the name given by psychologists to blind driving by individuals or groups over the highways of living. An experiment on 1,484 persons revealed that 96 per cent of them followed positively stated, false suggestions. Only 4 per cent of them were able to resist and think their ways through.

"If I had only stopped to think . . ." This well-known lament might be completed, ". . . I would not have acted on suggestion." To act on suggestion is to act without conscious thought. A very large portion of the snap judgments recently studied were made under the influence of suggestion. The parts of whole situations from which we see, hear, or otherwise sense and then rush to a conclusion are the *cues, tips,* or *hunches* upon which many people actually boast of acting.

The purpose of this discussion is to determine the ways in which one may increase conscious control over ideas and actions—in other words, to learn how to act less blindly, especially upon important occasions. All know the peril in driving

99

a car when the visibility is poor. Is it any wiser to go on blindly thinking or acting one's way through personal, business, or social affairs?

What is the source or cause of so much impulsive action—so much acting before thinking? For answer, attention is directed to some facts of human nature which were previously discussed. Attention has been called to the many strong instinctive and emotional drives toward the satisfaction of desires— hunger, thirst, curiosity, self-respect, and many others. The driving force of habit and tradition has also been studied. It has been noted, too, that individuals vary widely in their abilities to observe, remember, imagine, and resist emotional pressures. Out of this broad background of inheritance reinforced by habits, rises the problem of suggestion. The habits involved, of course, are deeply set long before the purpose, foresight, or reason of maturer years has had opportunity to play a large part in shaping conduct. Suggestion, therefore, takes deep root in human nature because such nature is made up of all the inherited and acquired characteristics and qualities of the individual.

INCREASING CONSCIOUS CONTROL

Why study the origin, the nature, and the influence of suggestion? Three very practical reasons may be given:

1. Everyone in active life has to face the necessity of influencing others. Some may call it *selling,* others may prefer to say *leadership,* while still others will employ the term *motivation.* How one may use the art of stimulating action on suggestion is presented by Ewer thus: "Suggestion is the natural or acquired art of the teacher, manager, advertiser, salesman, lawyer, physician, and clergyman. Likewise, in the unprofessional life of the home and shop, the method of securing ready belief and action without resort to the uncertain processes of argument is often desirable. . . . To present an idea, properly reinforced by suggested authority, sympathy, assurance, or fear—to command with sternness or to repeat with

tact—in other words, to play shrewdly upon the mental mechanisms of associates and subordinates is evidently a most valuable accomplishment."[1]

2. Another phase of this question is suggested in the discovery that in these days of high-pressure salesmanship there may be a need for many individuals to study the art of *resisting sales talk*.

3. Just as the driver is surer of reaching his destination safely when the visibility is good than when it is bad, it is obvious that the individual is more certain of his objectives if his conduct is *guided by thought* rather than by whim, impulses, or blind hunches.

However, in the process of deliberation, there is an important precaution. It seems to be a rule rather than an exception that one is not quite sure he is making the right decision, even after cool weighing of the evidence at his disposal. Choices must be made between job-offers, applicants, schools, trips, or even proposals of matrimony. In traveling through a district for the first time, a tourist pauses at an unmarked, complicated forking of the road. He tries to reason but soon becomes impatient with the lack of evidence. Impulsively, he follows a more confident-looking driver. Reason gives way to suggestion. People flip coins to avoid any appearance of being partial; but in making decisions about our lives, there are factors that should be shown partiality. To let flipped coins, drawn straws, imitation of others, and similar clues guide our lives for us is to relinquish our very self-direction.

Just as a study of one's own tendencies to look for insults where none is intended should safeguard an individual against taking undue offense, so an understanding of the influences leading to hasty action on suggestion should safeguard him against making a fool of himself. In any case, the student of suggestion stands to gain, whether he is a salesman eager to sell, or a prospective customer safeguarding his limited budget.

[1] Ewer, B. C., *Applied Psychology*. New York: The Macmillan Co.

GOVERNING PRINCIPLES

Hereafter are listed some principles which underlie the broad field of suggestion. The person who needs to influence others will do well to absorb their meaning and make every application of them that he can. Again, the person who needs to resist others will be aware of the areas in which to keep himself on guard.

1. *Count on the basic and secondary drives and appetites to work in their usual ways.* These may often be played upon to the advantage of the suggestor. Why does an advertisement of an overhead crane show a bathing beauty standing in the hook?

2. *Word your suggestion in such a way that your communication is successful.* This, of course, is the key to why so many people fail in trying to lead, teach, or influence others. Success requires proficiency in grammar, a good vocabulary, an understanding of what people are like and why they behave as they do, plus some shrewd judgment. Words sometimes have a way of accomplishing things that their speaker did not intend. Lecturers on salesmanship find a way to laughter and applause through telling of the novice who approached his first prospect with, "You don't want to take out a $5,000 policy today, do you?" The prospect is almost certain to reply, "No, not today." The salesman put the words into the prospect's mouth. Why blame the customer for repeating them? This is called *negative suggestion*; depending on the persons involved, it can sometimes be used to accomplish desired ends.

3. *Count on the individual to act in his habitual way.* A stimulus situation sets up a reaction tendency in the nervous system that will follow habit paths unless it is checked or redirected by conscious thought. A driver, accustomed to lighting his cigarettes with matches and then tossing the match out the window, uses his new lighter and then tosses it out the window. The child talks aloud in school; why not?—he was urged

to do so at home. The person whose reading experience is limited may whisper or work his lips as his eyes follow the printed symbols.

4. *Get the individual's interest.* To gain an individual's interest, one must learn his desires and his environmental and experiential backgrounds. This is what the wise salesman does before he calls on a prospective customer; then there is a common ground upon which to open conversation.

5. *Get the individual's concentrated attention.* Concentrated attention is essential before an individual or a group will act unconsciously on suggestion. A most striking illustration of this is found in hypnotism. By the hypnotist's skill and the subject's co-operation, the hypnotist secures the subject's undivided attention and then by various devices holds it on the bright spot or the single idea that he smoothly and monotonously repeats. Attention becomes fatigued, and the subject falls into an hypnotic sleep, losing his ordinary powers of self-direction. The spellbound audience has its attention deeply concentrated and may be said to be in the first stages of hypnotism.

6. *Display the mood you wish the individual to feel.* Mood begets mood. Action to be imitated or instructions to be immediately followed must be, or seem to be, spontaneous. Coolness is likely to be imitated or followed by coolness; deliberation, by deliberation. The college cheerleader, the group song-leader, and other "pep" rousers illustrate the natural imitation of impulsive actions.

7. *Conduct yourself the way in which you wish the individual to conduct himself. The Psychology of Military Leadership,* a text for officer training during World War II, stresses *indirect suggestion.* At all times the force of suggestion is determined by the way the officer speaks or acts. "In addition to words as tools of suggestion, body movements are loaded with it. Men through past experience are so accustomed to responding to others that the actions of the officer serve to arouse similar behavior in them. . . . The officer who stands with

drooping posture when calling soldiers to attention is counter-
acting his own order through the suggestion conveyed by his
stance."

In the light of what has been said, is suggestibility in an individual good or bad? Two review illustrations may make
the answer clearer. Emotion colors and enlivens personality;
but emotion misdirected or "running wild" ruins health, judgment, and human accomplishment. Consciousness of the causes
of bad judgment does not make an individual indecisive; it
rather speeds up his reliable perception. In the same way, an
intelligent understanding of the principles and laws of suggestion should leave the individual alert, sociable, and open
minded. He should be able to respond to ideas spontaneously
without being gullible and be able to respond to requests without jumping off bridges on sudden commands to do so.

Problem I

*State from case situations some of the principles or laws govern-
ing action on suggestion.*

CASE 1

1. Three suggestions were tried on a man about to leap to death
from a ledge 18 stories above the street. A woman first asked if she
might get him a cup of coffee. It didn't work. She then suggested
a glass of wine. Still the man was not influenced. As a third suggestion the woman cried: "You look *silly* on that ledge! Get down
before your wife sees you making a *fool* of yourself!" He got down
promptly.[2]

2. In one plant the foreman approaches a goggleless worker and
quietly places a glass eye on the bench beside him, remarking that
it is a nice color match and that the worker doubtless will need it
soon.

3. An effective speaker opens his talk with a question, a story,
or, even better, with a deliberate pause, as if weighing his words
very carefully before beginning.

[2] Wheeler, Elmer, *Tested Sentences That Sell.* New York: Prentice-Hall, Inc.

Case 2

A teacher once lost her voice for a day and afterward confessed that it was the best day of her teaching experience. She had to set up interesting activities to divert attention from mischief-makers instead of nagging, scolding, threatening, wheedling, or using other negative words creating antagonisms.

Case 3

"A housewife may be figuring her household accounts, directing her mental stream urgently in one direction, when suddenly a vague idea enters her mind that her hair needs adjustment. Automatically her hand goes up to her head and tucks in a hairpin. She continues her work uninterruptedly, and probably does not know that she has made the movement." [3]

Case 4

The expert gossip introduces his "news" or his subject with such expressions as, "Don't let this go any further, but . . ."; "I don't want to do Charlie any harm—he's one of my best friends, but . . ."; "I hate to say so, but . . ."; "Oh, by the way. . . ."

Case 5

1. We tend to accept readily, and without questioning, the word of an "expert."
2. "Imported."

Case 6

1. A supervisor or a recognized older workman takes it upon himself to stop to pick up a tool from the floor and put it in its place or throw a scrap of loose paper into the nearest wastebasket. Then others tend to look to cleanliness and order around their own aisles or workbenches.
2. In an unguarded moment, X tends to answer B's ill-tempered question in the same tone in which the question is asked.

Case 7

1. A reward for a man who could fry an egg without thinking of the word "hippopotamus" went unclaimed.
2. "Now children, don't put beans in your noses while I am gone."

[3] Kitson, H. D., *The Mind of the Buyer.* New York: The Macmillan Co.

CASE 8

An executive once said, "I never miss an opportunity to have my men in the shop hear me say that we have the best gang in the company, the best in safety, the best costs, the best place."

Problem II

Choose between ways of stating suggestions or asking questions.

CASE 1

1. The chances are only one to four that you'll lose.
2. The chances are four to one that you'll win.

CASE 2

1. When are you going to pay this bill?
2. Are you going to pay this bill?

CASE 3

1. Keep coming—you've got what it takes!
2. Snap out of it—you look all in!

CASE 4

1. Recommended by his superintendent.
2. Recommended by his foreman.

CASE 5

1. Would you have time to go swimming this afternoon?
2. How'd you like a good swim this afternoon? Come on!

CASE 6

1. Here's a good book I should like to have you read.
2. [Leaves book on workbench where boys may see it as they are working.]

CASE 7

1. Don't throw stones at the windows or write on the walls.
2. How long can we keep the building looking new and clean?

CASE 8

1. Roll up your sleeves before starting work.
2. Avoid working with loose sleeves in your way.

CASE 9

1. Do not lay tools on the bed of your lathe.

2. Lay lathe tools on tray to keep them free from chips and grease.

3. Lathe trays are there to keep tools free from chips and grease.

UNIT IX

Factors in Conduct

Objectives

1. *To recognize that there are causes of conduct.*
2. *To learn to search for the causes of conduct.*
3. *To identify the areas where causes may be found.*
4. *To recognize that the modification of causes may result in the modification of behavior.*

INTRODUCTION

"It is a horrible condemnation of our civilization," says one writer, "that technical knowledge has advanced to the point where its achievements border on the miraculous, while our knowledge of man has remained at almost medieval level. Tremendous bridges, skyscrapers, tunnels, airplanes, and what not, are designed and built with the greatest precision. We can predict with astounding accuracy future events in the astronomical universe, but we can scarcely make a beginning in shaping the lives of the individuals who are to use them." [1]

How can we account for this lag in understanding and dealing with human shortcomings? Much of the answer may be found in the theories or beliefs men have held as to the causes of human conduct. Not too long ago all acts were attributed to good or evil spirits. A mentally deranged person was "possessed of a devil" and often was cast out to starve or was stoned to death. Then there was the fatalistic theory. For example, if "it were intended" that John Smith was to slip on an oily floor and injure himself, that would happen to him in spite

[1] Langer, W. C., *Psychology and Human Living*. New York: D. Appleton-Century Co.

of anything he or anyone else might do. Again, as the science of biology advanced, heredity was seized upon as an explanation of human conduct. Since bodily characteristics were handed down according to well-known and predictable laws, ways of behaving were also said to come to an individual from his ancestors. Finally, there was the theory of *free will*. At every turn of a man's life he wills to do this or that of his own free choice. Few ever questioned the *causes* of his choice.

According to three of the above theories, the individual is the victim of influences over which he has no control. In the fourth, he is in complete control of every possible influence. Neither idea is very realistic.

THEORY OF CAUSATION

In sharp contrast to the superstitious, the fatalistic, or the mysterious explanations of human actions and attitudes that have held sway in the past, is a suggestion of the study of the causes of conduct with a view to modifying or preventing unfavorable effects. This cause-and-effect relationship may be called *determinism* if we keep in mind the fact that the term as used here refers to causes as determiners of reactions. *Causation* might be a better name for this modern theory of human behavior, since the word directly suggests inquiry into the influences leading up to the conduct in question.

This modern, enlightened point of view involves three major steps:

1. Establishing the attitude of assuming that there is a cause, or, as is more commonly the case, a set, or combination, of causes, underlying any conduct of an individual.

2. Conducting a cool and open-minded search for such causes.

3. Trying to remove the causes, or else moving the individual out of the range of influence of the causes of his difficulties. The first step is thoroughly possible in all cases, and in addition, is extremely important for two very definite reasons:

In the first place, if the supervisor, the teacher, the parent, or the student will only develop the habit of assuming that there may be hidden physical, habitual, environmental, or purely circumstantial causes back of the words or actions that irritate him, he has taken a long step in the direction of better personal relationships. He may not be able to find the causes of the other fellow's conduct; even if he finds the causes, he may not be able to do anything about them. Yet, the fact that he assumes that there must be a reason will, in most cases, prevent the rampage of temper, the snap judgment, or other hasty action that tends to make dealing with human situations ineffective or even injurious. When one learns to think in terms of cause and effect, his battle is half won.

In the second place, the fact-finding attitude of approaching a person constitutes the surest passkey with which to open up the source of his troubles. "Jump on him" and he will draw within his shell because of resentment or fear or both, and then any light he may be able to throw on the problem is lost. The very facts being looked for are buried.

What one names this modern theory of human conduct is unimportant. The thing that counts is the thoughtful habit of asking *why*. The saying, "We *feel* all the time, and *think* only part of the time," may be relatively true. However, through the building of constructive attitudes, the amount of conscious self-direction can be increased. And self-direction must precede or accompany successful influencing of the actions and attitudes of others.

The following discussion illustrates the method of application of this principle to problems of dealing with people. If an individual's reactions are undesirable, the question becomes one of throwing about him other influences favorable to more desirable conduct. *Blame* and *punishment* are thus sidetracked, and *re-education*, or *reconditioning*, takes their place. Punishment may still have a place as a means of discipline, but it is secondary in importance to such positive means as improvement of health, of motivation, of environment, or the clearing up of misunderstandings.

It is not uncommon for people to laugh at beliefs or practices of the past while holding to present theories with no more foundation. According to a news dispatch, poor-bearing fruit trees belonging to a certain tribe were subjected to severe lashings, with an admonition that they do better next season. Peasants of the region believe that the trees require punishment when they do not bear well. After native dances and other formalities, a score of the best specimens of tribal manhood administer ten lashes each to more than fifty trees.

There was a time when all inanimate objects were held accountable. If a man tripped over a chair and injured himself, then the chair was responsible and had to be punished by being broken up or burned. Until comparatively recent times, animals were held accountable for injuries they committed. A pig that broke into a neighboring garden might be hung in sight of the other pigs in order to be an example to them.

It becomes clear that the theories of individuals in any organization regarding the extent to which people are directly or consciously responsible for their acts, or the motives behind their acts, constitute a major factor in personnel relations in that organization. Tolerance, justice, and effective training depend very largely upon the appreciation and understanding of the more or less hidden causes upon which the conduct of people is based. Are they to be *blamed* and *punished?* Are they to be pushed aside as hopeless victims of circumstance? Or, are they to be *understood* and *aided?*

An individual may take the attitude toward his own failings that he has been victimized by circumstances or by heredity, or he may overlook his faults entirely, or he may take an intelligent inventory of himself and set to work to build up more constructive modes of behavior. He may be blind to his faults and weakly and passively blame himself, or he may initiate a self-training program according to the degree of his understanding of the causes of his own conduct.

WHERE TO LOOK FOR CAUSES

All of the possible influences that limit or determine an individual's conduct in any given situation will fall into the few areas of classification listed below. If the student will ask himself in each classification to just what extent the individual is *to blame,* he may arrive at the conclusion that "bawling out" and other forms of hasty "discipline" are about as intelligent and useful as slamming the door that bumps his head or kicking the cat upon whose toes he steps. These six classifications of causes of human behavior can be easily illustrated by the student, especially if he is a member of a discussion group:

1. *Basic and secondary drives.* (See Unit I.)
2. *Inherited abilities or inabilities.* (Aptitudes, physical characteristics, keenness of sense perception, etc.)
3. *Bodily conditions.* (Health, hunger, fatigue, etc.)
4. *Past environment.* (Training, general background.)
5. *Present environment.* (Physical and social.)
6. *Circumstances of the moment.* (Specific happenings rising out of the present environment.) Realization that there are causes beyond the individual's immediate control for the lack of proper performance or for acts that are positively harmful certainly does not mean that such acts are to be ignored or "put up with." But the employer will not *punish* the faulty worker—he will retrain him if he can, or he will put him where he can perform satisfactorily, if retraining does not seem reasonably possible. The state will not impose punishment upon the chronic offender if he is incompetent—it will take steps to recondition him or to isolate him so that he cannot injure others.

The primary purpose of this discussion is to call serious, deliberate attention to the many far-reaching, determining influences that still, in the main, govern the conduct of people. A thoughtful study of these should not only contribute to the betterment of human relations but should also advance the individual student in his own progress toward higher goals of constructive self-direction.

Problem I

In the following cases, and in other situations which you may have in mind, point out causes and possible preventive or curative measures.

CASE 1

1. A pieceworker suffered a nervous breakdown resulting in prolonged disability because, after repeated *warnings*, she was unable to develop the speed required to make the standard rate that others were making easily.

2. Judd was a hard worker, but he dropped out of school because his parents and his teachers ridiculed him for getting lower grades in Latin and English than his younger sister did.

CASE 2

A boy quit his first job suddenly and to the great surprise and regret of his employer. All his life the boy had heard from his father and elder brothers the doctrine, "take nothing off anybody." A very mild "calling down" from his employer earlier in the day had so worked upon the boy's conscience, conditioned as it was by the ideals set up for him by his elders, that he felt he would be violating the traditions of the entire family if he took this imagined insult. He really wanted to stay, but his conscience compelled him to quit.

CASE 3

A wheel of the truck hit a loose casting in the aisle, and the load of small parts rattled to the floor.

"What th'—did you do that for?" shouted the foreman.

"What th'—do you suppose?" was the immediate comeback from the young trucker.

CASE 4

After reprimanding a telephone equipment assembler several times because of errors in placement of wires in assembling color-coded cables, the foreman discovered that the worker was color blind, and that the worker himself was not aware of his own vision defect.

CASE 5

A defective steering mechanism causes one motorist to collide with another.

CASE 6

Burnham reports the case of a young cashier in a store who was sent to a psychiatrist for examination because of her many errors in making change. Examinations revealed that she was undernourished, slow, inaccurate, but had fair learning ability and a good personality. Her home situation was unhappy. She was a failure as a cashier, but her pleasant personality indicated that she might succeed in sales work. She was then transferred to the house furnishings department. The psychiatrist advised her regarding her home life and helped her work out a plan for her leisure time. Her health improved. At the time of the report, she was showing alertness, aggressiveness, and self-confidence, and she was being tried out for promotion to head of stock, a position for which there was keen competition.

CASE 7

Seventy-five years ago a little Swiss girl in a village school was whipped daily because she would not read—whipped, scolded, and placed upon a high stool with a dunce cap on her head. From the stool near the blackboard she learned to read, evidence, you see, that the discipline was needed. Her vision was defective, and from her own seat in the schoolroom she could not see the characters on the board. Later, as an adult, science came to her aid and she acquired glasses.

One cannot brush aside this story on the ground that such things do not happen today, for they do. Teachers no longer punish myopic children for their inability to see, but in all good faith foremen, supervisors, and employers in general accept handicapped persons for work which they cannot do, and administer disciplinary discharges, which are the equivalent of whippings, when they fail.[2]

CASE 8

You have often heard a teacher say of a pupil that he is "bright for his age." This is just what is meant by the psychologist who

[2] Pond, Millicent, "The Future of Employment Tests." *Industrial Relations,* October, 1932.

tells you that your boy "has a high I. Q." The letters, *I. Q.*, stand for "intelligence quotient," and represent a comparison of the child's mental age with his chronological age. Thus the 7-year-old who can do the mental tasks of a 9-year-old has an I. Q. of 9 divided by 7, or 129 on a percentage basis.

The answer becomes clear, however, when it is understood what psychologists mean by intelligence and mental age. Intelligence, as the term is used precisely by scientists, does not include education, or skill, or the "wisdom" gained as a result of experience in the world. It is rather the innate capacity to understand, the ability to profit from experience, that distinguishes the bright person from the stupid one. A dull adult may know a great deal more (have more factual information) than a bright child, yet he may be less intelligent.[3]

CASE 9

Louise, a brilliant freshman college girl, was sullen and remained in her room practically all the time outside recitation hours. She seemed to be annoyed when other students called upon her and she would have nothing to say. She is now ignored by them. Inquiry into her past history would have revealed that as a very small child she would often cry if people spoke to her; that she was brought up by an indulgent grandmother who never allowed her to play with other children; that she was a "grind" in high school and had been left alone to her studies and introspections since her first year there.

[3] Van de Water, Marjorie, in the *Rochester Democrat and Chronicle.*

UNIT X

Personality

Objectives

1. *To recognize those components of personality which are under the individual's own control.*
2. *To recognize the possibilities of modifying personality through purposeful self-direction.*
3. *To formulate individual programs of personality growth that will best serve the personal needs of each individual.*

INTRODUCTION

Personality is usually described in terms of all the traits or reaction tendencies affecting the social adjustment of the individual. Social adjustment simply means getting along harmoniously with people. Here are several representative definitions of, or references to, personality:

1. "By personality we mean the extent to which one is able to interest or influence other people." [1]

2. "Personality is what you do when you are with other people. It is an activity, not a possession." [2]

3. "Interpreting personality is a matter of discovering attitudes. Is a man conceited or depreciatory as he views himself? Is he interested or bored as he discharges the duties of his job? Is he co-operative or individualistic in his social relations? Is he obedient or rebellious toward those in authority? Is he optimistic or pessimistic as he faces the future? The answers to such questions tell the story of the real man." [3]

---

[1] Link, H. C., *Rediscovery of Man.* New York: The Macmillan Co.
[2] Bernreuter, R. G. (Pennsylvania State College).
[3] Vaughan, W. F., *Op. cit.*

116

4. "As a house is built of separate stones, bricks, and timbers, so our personalities are built of a conglomeration of muscular, emotional, and verbal habits." [4]

The modern tendency is to look upon personal growth, or personality, as a rich by-product of well-directed activity, rather than as a conscious goal within itself. Given such attitudes and opportunities as pride in the job, interest in employers and employees, and participation in a healthful range of group activities, growth of personality will take care of itself.

BASIC NEEDS

If it is true that an individual's personality at any given time in his life is the result of his efforts to satisfy his needs with the aid of such native abilities, insights, incentives, and counseling as he may have had, is it not important for supervisors, parents, teachers, and other leaders to consider carefully these broad human needs that lie back of life's activities?

Prescott, in one of the most thorough studies into the emotions or motives of human activity, discusses "basic personality needs" under three headings: [5]

1. *Physical needs.* Requirements for air, food, and liquids, clothing and shelter, activity and rest, relaxation and play.

2. *Social needs.* That he may have "an unassailable feeling of his own value," the individual needs such possessions as affection, sense of "belonging" in groups, feeling that he is well thought of, and that in essential matters he is like other human beings.

3. *Personal needs* (personal recognition). ". . . because personality development requires activity in ever-widening social spheres and involves a steadily increasing number of materials, machines and forces, the individual cannot fail to evaluate himself in terms of his effectiveness in dealing with social and material situations."

---

[4] Walton, Albert, *Fundamentals of Industrial Psychology.* New York: McGraw-Hill Book Co.

[5] Prescott, D. A., *Op. cit.*

Prescott takes pains to explain that specific classification of such life forces is merely a matter of convenience in studying them; that no one of these needs is ever the sole driving force uninfluenced by the others in the life of an individual; and that they are not set forth as being either wholly instinctive or wholly acquired. It is for forces such as these that the student of human nature is looking in planning effective incentives.

It may be assumed that the slant or point of view from which personality is studied in this course is that of its bearing on leadership. All desirable personalities may not be leaders, but all real leaders must have effective personalities. To play his part in the manufacture or the distribution of any kind of product or service, the supervisor must keep people working cooperatively and effectively. This ability is the basic test of personality.

FACTORS UNDER ONE'S CONTROL

Psychologists have a vocabulary of scientific terminology that has grown out of their extensive investigation of the phenomena of personality. The terms and the concepts that are so useful to the psychologists and the psychiatrists are of relatively little use to the "man in the street" and, for that reason, will not be found in this discussion. However, there are certain definite components of the total personality that have strong influence upon other people and that are decidedly under an individual's own control. These are listed under eight major headings:

1. *Appearance.* The first personality factors to impress themselves upon one in meeting an individual are those of a visual nature, such as size, build, posture, features, dress, grooming, etc. In pointing to a picture of a prisoner, a physician in a penitentiary once said, "When that man came in here, all he had for a nose was a mere lump on his face—no bridge at all. We put him on the operating table, removed the end of a floating rib, and built him up a nose. You see this picture.

Now look at a picture of him when he came here! His personality is completely changed! If he had looked this way before, he probably would have held a good position, and would not have committed crime."

2. *Mental alertness.* As one talks to the intelligent individual, physical defects tend to disappear. The prejudiced saying, "Beauty and brains don't go together," is being disproved by study, and it is being found that the argument to the effect that the person of fine mind cannot be called ugly is more nearly accurate. It does not make nearly as much difference how intelligent you are as how awake, alive, and "on the beam" you are with whatever intelligence you have.

3. *Habits or learning.* This covers all the things you do— your activities—above all, your *manners.* Fidgety little mannerisms come under this heading too; they can be important factors in someone's personality picture.

4. *Interest in others.* If you are bothered by self-consciousness, Dr. Robert G. Bernreuter would tell you that you are conscious of the wrong person, and that the way to help yourself is to practice being more conscious of other people around you by directing your thinking toward them. When someone is telling you experiences that are *interesting to him,* do you tend to break in with your stories that are of interest to *you?* Are you a good listener?

5. *Sociability.* Sociability grows out of a combination of habits, learning, and interest in others. It warrants separate consideration in that it consists of a whole group of reactions and behaviors that together make up what is called *outreach* to others. This can be cultivated as a technique even if it is not sincerely felt.

6. *Emotional warmth and stability.* This is sometimes called *temperament,* and has already been given considerable attention in this course.

7. *Attitudes.* Does the individual tend to be aggressive or retiring? Are his interests broad or narrow? Is he forward-looking or lacking in purpose? Does he tend to throw himself into the

job with enthusiasm, or does he seem to gripe or knock? Is he open-minded or is he prejudiced?

8. *Purposeful self-direction.* Perhaps the old and generally misunderstood term *will power* has not been given enough specific consideration. A terse, clear, modern definition of will power is, "A man's habitual way of formulating and carrying out a course of action." [6] This habitual way of carrying on is simply a part or characteristic of an individual's conduct. There are three steps in the activity: *resolution, initiative,* and *persistence.* A person resolves on a plan, initiates it, and persists until it is finished. Instead of the older idea that *will* was some mysterious talent or power that one happened by nature to have or not to have, *will* is now looked upon as the effect of causes which may be determined, removed, or strengthened. This purposeful self-direction is subject to the same kind of intelligent control or redirection as is any other kind of habit.

It is impossible to emphasize too much the fact that the above eight personality factors are items over which a person has *almost complete control.* Within reasonable limitations a person can, by working on himself in these areas, tailor for himself almost any kind of personality he wishes.

The leader stands or falls on his effectiveness in influencing the behavior of others—directing, interesting, co-ordinating, teaching, checking, rating, promoting, and rewarding. The real leader of any group may not be the one who is out in front. The test of his leadership is the degree to which his plans are being carried out by his group. He may, in the main, direct by making quiet suggestions that others grasp and make their own. His chief interest is in *results* rather than in *credit.* Then, when credit does come, it comes with telling force.

---

[6] Pennington, L. A., Hough, R. B., and Case, H. W., *The Psychology of Military Leadership.* New York: Prentice-Hall, Inc.

Problem I

How is personality development related to work?

CASE 1

The lack of proper character traits and not lack of specific skill is responsible for both firing and for lack of advancement. Most of the causes, 89.9 per cent, given for termination of employment are in character traits, while only 10.1 per cent are for lack of skill. [H. Chandler Hunt's survey covering every type of industry and employing 49,854 clerical workers.] Hunt listed as the ten most common causes for loss of jobs: carelessness, nonco-operation, absence from work for reasons other than illness, dishonesty, attention to things other than office work during office hours, lack of initiative, lack of ambition, lack of loyalty.

CASE 2

With the exception of the time a person spends in bed, the ordinary adult spends more of his life in a plant, factory, or place of business than anywhere else. While other situations may produce more highly colored emotional experiences, none of them has the continuity and stability as a stimulating background for the worker's thought and action than has a man's place of work. We may rightfully expect, therefore, that the work environment will color a man's thoughts, determine his habits, crystallize his attitudes, facilitate or inhibit physical and mental health, and increase or decrease the effectiveness of his general social adjustment.[7]

CASE 3

We must interest or influence other people in getting a job or a raise in salary, in making and keeping friends. In business, in government, and in all the social relationships, a good mind or a good character is handicapped unless coupled with an effective personality. This ability to influence other people is made up of habits and skills acquired by practice. An awkward boy who, by persistent effort, has learned a fair game of tennis, has acquired thereby one set of personality habits which enables him to interest and influence other boys.

Neither tennis nor any other one game or skill is necessary to a good personality, but a range and variety of acquired skills are.[8]

[7] Stevens, S. N., American Management Association *Prod. Series, No. 119.*

[8] Link, Henry C., *Reader's Digest*, December, 1936.

Case 4

The late George Herbert Palmer of Harvard is credited with the widely quoted sentiment to the effect that he was getting paid for doing work which he gladly would do without pay.

How many people are proud of the work they are doing?

Is it the exception or the rule that people find something in connection with their work to "brag" about?

How does enthusiasm influence personal advancement? Health? Personality?

Case 5

In looking around for an understudy or "right-hand man" how would you like to find this chap?

He doesn't need much supervision—likes to lend a hand—has a reputation for getting things done—does more than "his part" when needed.

He seems to be looked upon as a leader—others often ask his opinion or his advice—"my mistake" comes easily when he does make an error.

He appreciates the problems of management and supervision.

He makes his desires for advancement clear, but maintains poise and perspective if promotions do not come with the tick of the clock—has the "Rome was not built in a day" attitude.

Problem II

How are human attitudes involved in dealing with people? How are they acquired? How may they be changed? How do they influence personality?

Case 1

An illustration of a relatively simple attitude is found in the crouching position of a cat watching a mouse hole and ready to spring upon its intended victim. In this instance, the attitude is a motor set and its accompanying state of visceral tension; functionally it is a condition of preparation for overt action. A complex human attitude is illustrated by an individual with some pronounced and fixed political bias. Psychologically the two cases have much in common. In both, the attitude is a reaction tendency which involves practically the entire physiological equipment of the organism concerned.[9]

CASE 2

Kilpatrick says: "When two things have happened together in experience, the thought of one tends to call up the other. . . . Most emotional nature furnishes fear as a way of responding. What we actually fear seems to come entirely by this association. We learn by it our particular fears. Likes and dislikes also come largely in this way. A man of established professional standing confessed to the writer his aversion to a certain color on a book cover because this had been a boyhood association with a distasteful high school course. . . . Anything we work with, whatever it may be, presents different phases and has varied connection. With each of these phases or connections, some emotional attitude is in a greater or less degree associated. . . . Out of these mounting attendant attitudes, their concomitant learnings, come in time life's effectual attitudes now grown so strong as to dominate from within the emotional and volitional outlook." [10]

CASE 3

Especially in regard to conventional thought, belief, custom, and the like, an unconscious influence appears. Freedom from this slavery in the case of certain superior men seems to have been the condition that made great discoveries possible. This apparently furnished a bit of evidence for the view that the genius owes his superiority, not so much to greater ability, as to freedom from inhibitions by which other men are handicapped.[11]

CASE 4

Wheeler says: "Students who have not acquired a scientific attitude before they become of college age will not find this attitude easy of attainment during the brief exposure furnished by a beginning course in psychology. Yet for an adequate grasp of the spirit, purpose, method, and facts of psychology, the acquisition of such an attitude is essential. *First,* a scientific investigator should approach his subject matter with open and unprejudiced mind but at the same time in a spirit of questioning, criticism, and doubt.

[9] Perrin, F. A. C., and Klein, D. R., *Psychology.* New York: Henry Holt and Company.
[10] Kilpatrick, W. H., *Education for a Changing Civilization.* The Century Co.
[11] Stribling, T. S., *The Unfinished Cathedral.* Doubleday, Doran and Co.

Facts and theories alike should not be accepted merely on the basis of authority without an independent attempt to ascertain their reasonableness. *Second,* an investigator should be persevering. Many are the problems which will require prolonged concentration on this task. *Third,* any investigator should exercise all the caution and precision in technique and thinking which he has at his command. He should not come to conclusions hastily or be certain of his facts until they have been carefully verified." [12]

Problem III
Distinguish three separate elements in purposeful self-direction.

CASE 1
Convinced that the earth was a sphere, Columbus resolved to reach the East by sailing west. He secured financial support and enlisted a crew:

> Behind him lay the gray Azores,
>   Behind the Gates of Hercules;
> Before him not the ghost of shores,
>   Before him only shoreless seas.
> The good mate said: "Now must we pray,
>   For lo! the very stars are gone.
> Brave Admiral, speak, what shall I say?"
>   "Why say, 'Sail on! sail on! and on!' " [13]

CASE 2
What qualities, or abilities, or lack of abilities, are suggested by the phrases, "straddling the fence," "self-starter," and "bulldog grit"?

Problem IV
Formulate rules for increasing the efficiency of one's own responses.

CASE 1
Know your strong point and play it.

[12] Wheeler, R. H., *The Science of Psychology.* Thomas Y. Crowell Co.
[13] Miller, Joaquin, *Columbus,* vs. 1.

Case 2

A co-operative student said, "I am going to review my 'math' during my month at work." He didn't do much. Another said, "I'm going to work two problems in each exercise that we have gone over during the past month." He did it.

Case 3

"Second thought" arrives too late to be of help to many a hot-head, but it will begin to be more prompt as a result of thoughtful study of the history and the results of one's troublesome psychology.

Case 4

New paths are made easy to follow by frequent and consistent use; old ones are easily reopened by a little retraveling.

Case 5

A small boy in Kansas observed that his dog could catch the swiftest rabbit that hopped the prairies if only one rabbit were scared up at a time. But, if two or more rabbits sprang from their hiding places, all would escape the speedy dog because he would hesitate too long in picking his victim.

Case 6

One of the commonest causes of trouble with algebra is the feeling of the student that he should see the solution or the entire way to the solution before beginning work on the problem.

Case 7

Steady fixation of the mind on California gold kept many a pioneer on the dry and dusty trail until he arrived in the "Land of Promise."

Case 8

Muscles that are not used become soft, flabby, and incapable of obeying the will effectively.

UNIT XI

Counseling and Placement

Objectives

1. To check reliability of reasoning leading to selection of career goals.
2. To focus attention upon the many handicaps in early life that can be removed by discovery and prompt action. School and work difficulties often give the clues to such needs.
3. To understand better the close tie-up of interests between foremen, employees, and employment managers in the employment process.
4. To consider counseling as an opportunity and an obligation upon leaders in all walks of life—home, school, business, community.

INTRODUCTION

Counseling refers to the aid which one person (the counselor) gives to another (the counselee) in making a satisfactory adjustment to a problem. It is the purpose of all guidance or counseling to "—build the happiest, most fully integrated personality possible upon the foundation which nature and previous experience have provided the individual." [1] It is not to be inferred from this definition that specific directions should be given by one person to another. The individual must make his own decisions—must progress along his own chosen route of counseled self-direction. It is for this reason that persons in the field today speak of *counseling* instead of *guidance*.

A counselor's primary duty is twofold. He must first help the counselee gain insight into his problem—to recognize and face it as it exists. Not until a problem is clearly understood and

[1] Trabue, M. R., *Recent Developments in Testing for Guidance.* Review of Educational Research.

126

squarely faced can steps be taken to solve it. It is in this aspect of counseling that feelings and attitudes are dealt with. Second, the counselor must be able to give specific information where it is needed. This may include the nature, educational requirements, necessary training, and opportunities of various occupations. Or, it might concern such factors as the offerings and entrance requirements of educational institutions.

These are basic to all types of counseling. Specific functions are dependent upon the type of assistance needed by the individual. There are several major types of counseling, which are to be discussed below. It must be remembered, however, that there is much overlapping between them. Human problems are complex, and it is seldom that only a single aspect of a person's life is involved in the counseling procedure.[2] The experienced counselor is prepared to handle problems of a multiform nature.

AREAS OF COUNSELING

Vocational counseling, as the term implies, refers to counseling for a vocation—assisting a person in the selection of a trade, profession, or some other type of occupation. To do this, it is important that the counselor know the counselee's interests, aptitudes and achievements, and temperament and cultural background. It is also important that the counselor be aware of the skills and training required and the physical demands of various lines of work. The wise occupational counselor will present this information to the individual and let him make his own decisions. Though exceptions undoubtedly exist, one can probably say that in general the more limited a person's native abilities and intellectual capacity, the more specific and directional guidance may be.

Educational counseling is concerned with helping the student select, and assure himself that he is making, the proper preparation for his chosen occupation. As aids in assisting the

[2] Paterson, D. G., Schneidler, G. G., and Williamson, E. G., *Student Guidance Techniques*. New York: McGraw-Hill Book Co., Inc.

student, the counselor makes use of testing programs, course or work achievement records, behavior records, and any other pertinent information at his disposal. The counselor must help the individual evaluate his progress and his suitability for any proposed program of study.

Personal counseling (emotional and social) deals most directly with feelings and attitudes—frequent causes of job or educational failure. Such failure, in turn, may aggravate emotional problems. It is the duty of the counselor to clarify the individual's expressed feelings and make it possible for him to face problems squarely and do something about them. Satisfactory relationships with the social environment and use of leisure time are factors to be stressed in this aspect of counseling.

Health and economic counseling are also important phases that must not be overlooked. Retardation and social difficulties of the most serious nature have been due to recognized or unrecognized physical handicaps. Adenoids, malnutrition, harelips—these are merely suggestions of preventable causes of suffering and failure on the part of thousands of individuals. "Needlessly blind" were the words burned into the memory of an eminent educator of the blind when, as a child, she heard the physician who gave her an examination comment upon her case to the superintendent of the institution in whose care she had been placed. Financial worries have long been recognized as a possible cause of severe maladjustment. Scholarship and student loan funds, provisions for part-time work opportunities, and budgeting instructions are illustrations of the attention being paid to this kind of assistance.

From these brief descriptions of various types of counseling, it is apparent that it would be impossible to divorce and isolate them one from another. How is it possible for the educational counselor to avoid being also a vocational counselor? And how is it conceivable for any counselor to escape personal counseling when feelings and attitudes are an integral part of vocational and educational desires?

Counselors' Aids

Counselors make use of several types of tools as aids in the counseling process:

1. Of first importance is the interview. This is used to reveal problems, obtain relevant information, and define factors such as interests, hobbies, and skills.

2. Occupational and educational information are essential. One of the greatest aids here is the *Dictionary of Occupation Titles*, designed for use in the United States Employment Service.

3. The counselor makes use of anecdotal records or behavior journals and any other pertinent data concerning the individual. Counselors are discovering that leaders in industry, business, and the professions emphasize questions having to do with personality or character when they seek information about an individual whom they consider for employment or promotion. If these questions are to be answered to the best advantage of all, the counselor must have at his ready command reliable records of the individual's behavior over a substantial period of time. The title *behavior journal* is often used in schools for such an individual record. As the word "journal" suggests, the record contains chronological entries of facts, observations, comments, and diagnostic summaries. Each entry is a report of an episode in the life of a student—a word picture of the student in action or a characterization of him in a certain situation at a certain time.

4. The counselor also makes use of various psychological tests. These fall into several categories:

Interest inventories. Such are used to substantiate or point out discrepancies of stated interests and to reveal possible inclinations not consciously recognized by the counselee.

Intelligence tests. The true nature of "intelligence" is not as yet clearly understood, but such tests can reveal ability to deal with abstract or verbal materials as well as with concrete situations (*performance intelligence*).

Aptitude tests. Scholastic aptitude tests are much like the verbal tests referred to above, but are used mainly for predicting success in school work. Manual dexterity and ability to acquire skills demanded in clerical activities are illustrations of other kinds of individual possibilities revealed through aptitude testing.

Achievement tests. These are used to obtain a measure of accomplishment in any field in which the individual has had training.

Personality inventories. These attempt to give clues concerning an individual's feelings and attitudes, which go to make up his personality, and often are used to supplement or check the counselor's impressions resulting from the interview.

In summary, it should be emphasized that the purpose of all counseling is to help individuals make satisfactory adjustments to life problems, in order that they may live happy and productive lives. In counseling it is necessary to have knowledge of the individual's past and present environments and his manner of reacting to them: his attitudes, interests, aspirations, and particular ability. This information is essential and its meaning must be made manifest to the individual if the counseling process is to reach a satisfactory conclusion.

EMPLOYMENT POINT OF VIEW

The long depression period of the '30's tended to focus attention upon a neglected phase of good employment-office practice. "Certainly the finding of the right man for the job to be filled is as important today as it ever was," remarked the personnel manager of one of the country's largest manufacturing industries early in 1940, "but there is another important factor in employment office procedure that is receiving, and will continue to receive, increased consideration. Techniques must be developed that will create more constructive attitudes on the part of the applicant who cannot be offered employment promptly. He must be given a clearer understanding of his prospects and of the interest that others have in him. His courage must be sustained in times of economic stress when there are far more people seeking work than industry has the ability to absorb."

In order that there might be time for direct and friendly counseling for all comers, many industries materially *increased their employment interview staffs during the prewar years of unemployment*. Although there may never be any definite formulas written for the guidance of individuals looking for work where there is no work, some definite information, some proof of personal interest, and some practical understanding that these counselors in business and industry are in a key position to give are effective. It may be safe to predict that demands for this kind of service to individuals will increase as its value gains wider recognition, and that the statement of the personnel manager will be as vital in the future as it was in 1940.

Intramural personal counseling also is being given renewed consideration. Supervisors of all ranks are being trained to understand and deal with attitudes of older workers whose ways may be firmly established, as well as with younger workers who may have their attitudes confused and unsettled by abnormal conditions. Cases of supervisory counseling have already been discussed under many of the previous problems and cases in this course. The feature of this type of counseling today is that more conscious attention is being focused upon it.

The regular processes through which employees are selected and placed continue to retain their importance. One survey, reported in the *Personnel Journal,* ranks the selection and placement of workers as the first of five most important personnel problems. One local company follows a procedure that seems fundamentally sound. Applicants are interviewed and fill out an application form which is filed for ready reference. As vacancies develop applicants are called in for more detailed interviews. After the second interview, the applicant selected is sent to the department in which the vacancy exists.

Here he meets the foreman, may be interviewed briefly, and is shown the job on which he is to work and the working conditions surrounding the job. He usually meets some of his future fellow employees. Final selection of him is made by the departmental supervisor. Thus, the new employee has direct contact with the conditions under which he is to work, knows to whom he is to report, and meets, and is met by, his direct superior before accepting the job or being accepted for it.

After the applicant is accepted by the department, he is given a medical examination to determine not only his physical qualifications for industrial employment in general, but also to ensure his being placed on a job which he is physically able to do. If the report on this medical examination is satisfactory, the new employee is given information relating to safety, as well as other plant rules, and is told when to report.

STARTING THE NEW EMPLOYEE

When the new employee arrives for work the first day, he reports to his foreman, who in turn delegates someone from the department to introduce him to the job and to some of his immediate associates. At this point formal job training begins. Not many years ago the statement might have been accepted generally that the new man's success on the job depended approximately 25 per cent upon proper selection, 25 per cent upon proper placement, and 50 per cent upon adequate instruction and training. Today many thoughtful personnel men would accept this analysis only on the condition that the employee's immediate supervisor is able and willing to see to it that "adequate instruction and training" takes into full account the necessary reconditioning of attitudes toward work that recent economic conditions may have developed in the new employee.

The employee's progress on the job is affected both by the rating given his job and by the rating he is given in relation to other employees on his particular type of work. Job rating, or job evaluation, is obviously the responsibility of management. The first-line supervisor—the man in direct contact with the employee—is the one who must do the rating of the individual in relation to the work of others in his particular department. It is this foreman or direct supervisor who knows the employee's attitudes, responsibilities, judgment, leadership, and general effectiveness on the job.

This discussion has covered the responsibility of the employment manager to those applicants for whom there is no job available and has also traced some procedures through which a selected applicant goes in being located and trained on the job given him. As to the other requirement for selection and placement—namely, judging the qualifications of the prospective employee—there is a rapidly growing mass of materials and methods to aid in analyzing the possibilities of new men who are being considered. Through improved *application forms, job specifications,* and, sometimes, *tests,* information is assembled to assist the employment office in the central employing device, the *interview.*

The typical employment blanks call for name, address, dependents; height, weight, physical defects; education; friends or relatives employed in the establishment in which employment is sought; last employment—how long, reasons for leaving; other work applicant can do; references. All promising applicants fill out these blanks. When they are studied intelligently, they furnish valuable help not only in selection, but also in placement and transfer.

With an analysis of each job in his plant at hand, the employment interviewer can much more readily study a particular applicant's fitness for a specific position. The typical job analysis covers job description, supervision exercised by operator, judgment required as to quality of product, responsibility for material and equipment, manual dexterity, working conditions, hazards, physical and mental requirements, and learning period.

TESTING PROGRAMS

Intelligence tests, aptitude tests, and trade tests constitute another source of aid in employee selection. The consideration of such tests is not easily free of prejudice because of general misunderstanding regarding claims made for them. No psychologist of repute has claimed more for any series of tests than that they may be the means of securing additional evidence of a man's fitness for specific lines of employment. Results secured are weighed along with other evidences and undoubtedly make a highly worth-while contribution when they are administered by competent persons. In reviewing the problem of testing, a member of a Rochester employment department says:

"The use of psychological tests in industry is somewhat limited, and there is a definite danger in the use of test results by those who are not fully acquainted with the limitations and factors which may nullify them; however, they do have definite value when properly used.

"The application and the use of tests in industry and elsewhere should be preceded by extensive and objective experimentation and trial. Briefly, this means that nothing can be gained by using the result of a test without being able definitely to correlate test scores with objective measures of performance such as turnover, errors, and quantity performance. In a few instances, where these objective records do not exist, it may be possible to secure sufficiently objective ratings by supervision against which to check the test scores; but, more often than not, personal factors enter into these ratings to such an extent that they correlate very low with test factors regardless of how well established.

"Uncertainties regarding the correlation between job success and general intelligence test scores have resulted in the use primarily of *aptitude* tests and *trade* tests. Aptitude tests are those which, though of a performance nature, can be relied upon to give materially the same results regardless of training or practice. Manual dexterity, or speed of muscular reaction, for example, may be detected by standard test exercises regardless of the past experience of the person being tested. Trade tests measure degree of accomplishment and training in a given field, and the ultimate scores vary in direct relationship to proficiency. Trade tests are relatively easy to administer. They may vary all the way from verbal questions about tools used or other details of a job in which the applicant claims to have had experience to extensive performances to demonstrate proficiency."

THE INTERVIEW

Records of all types serve to make the *interview* more effective, and the latter remains the most important phase of the employment procedure. One of the most marked improvements of recent years is in the setting prepared for the employment interview. Cages, windows, and cramped and catchall types of employment offices are giving way to more spacious reception rooms with desks for interviewers where interviewer and interviewee may sit down for a comfortable talk. It will be readily recognized that the value of the interview depends primarily upon the character and training of the interviewer. Viteles discusses the training of interviewers under such headings as: Prepare Definite Questions to Ask; Know Your Field; Gain and Deserve Interviewee's Confidence; Practice Taking the Interviewee's Point of View; Listen; Be Straightforward and Frank Rather than Shrewd or Clever; Allow Time Enough; Get All the Facts; Check Results.[3]

The interview is not only a tool of the employment office, but it is also the *supervisor's* chief means of getting the facts he needs if he is to solve many of his personnel problems. The following four-point outline for interviewing applies directly to the supervisor:

1. *Listen* with patience and encouraging interest. Don't interrupt.

[3] Viteles, M. S., *Op. cit.*

2. *No hasty disapproval.* If what the employee is saying sounds disloyal or offensive, keep composed and look beyond his particular, heated remarks for the specific cause of his attitude.

3. *Don't argue.* Arguments fan the flame, and present attitudes are set so and are rarely changed by argument.

4. *Look for what the employee tries or wishes to say.* Find better ways of encouraging him, with such statements as "Go on." Ask questions that will help him think of, understand, or express his real ideas and feelings.[4]

The purpose of this outline for consideration by supervisors is that they may see how their own work represents the actual follow-up of personnel principles, the applications of which begin with the employee's first contacts with the company. Supervisors themselves have the responsibility of continuing, throughout the employee's years with the company, applications of the same principles. In fact, the supervisor's job is becoming more and more one of co-ordination of the work of many specialists. It would, in ordinary cases, be impossible, even if it were desirable, for the foreman to master the techniques of the employment manager, the air conditioning engineer, the time and motion study man, the director of training, etc. However, he can familiarize himself with the aims of these specialists, the place of each in the organization, and the points of contact between each and himself in order that he may give intelligent and open-minded co-operation to management and put organization-wide policies into practice.

The extent of progress made in employment in recent years is suggested by this vivid description of former practices:

"Those days we simply hired and fired," writes A. H. Young. "The process of hiring was as simple as the crooking of one's finger. When a foreman discovered a vacancy in his gang, he hied himself immediately to the main gate of the plant where a crowd was gathered seeking employment. Hastily glancing

[4] Roethlisberger, F. J., *Management and Morale.* Cambridge, Mass.: Harvard University Press.

over the throng, he would single out a likely looking prospect, beckon him with his finger, and say a few words in what we should term today a dead language, for in those early days he talked in terms of 12½ and 15 cents an hour. If it was a go, he simply told the man to get on the job, and the man was expected to know what to do by some kind of intuitive knowledge. When the timekeeper came around, the foreman told him the man's name, occupation, and rate. If the man's name was too involved because of foreign sound or spelling, it frequently happened that the new employee was christened on the spot, and today we still have on steelmill payrolls the Joe Dollars and Frank Pennies that marked the end (so far as the payrolls are concerned) of ancient Polish lineage. If the foreman was dissatisfied with the man's performance, there was no 'exit interview,' or anything of the kind. He was simply fired. If he wanted to argue the matter, the foreman, of course, had the privilege of telling him where to go; but usually, instead of going to one of those warmer regions, the employee took his place in the line at the gate the following morning and was frequently rehired by another foreman in the same manner. As a matter of fact, I know of one instance where the same man was hired and fired twenty-six times in the same plant within a year."

Problem I

How did individuals find their vocations before science took up the problem?

CASE 1

Joe Smith, eldest son of the family, became a farmer because he grew up in the work of helping his father run the place.

CASE 2

Tom Smith didn't like the farm because Joe assumed the role of boss and made him do all the drudgery. He went to town and took a job as a messenger because the pay was "good, for a kid." When he was no longer a "kid," he heard of a job at better pay in a mill. He is still going from job to job; his brother calls him a "hobo," and he has almost decided that he must have been "cut out for a hobo anyway."

CASE 3

Johnnie Jones, a village workman's son, listened to his neighbor's radio. Then he found in a catalogue luring advertisements of radio parts, with diagram and manual. He invested his savings with a mail-order house, built a little set, and became the pride of his parents and the talk of the neighborhood. All pronounced him a genius. As a result, he decided to become an electrical engineer. The object itself produced the desire, and the advertisement created interest, but neither of these, as later experience in school proved, was a reliable test of the boy's ability to master electrical theory.

CASE 4

Charles R., a small town banker's son, was interested in nothing so much as fancy poultry. But his father said that he had enough money to give his son the best education and that he wanted him to go into "an honorable profession." After years of urging and driving, the banker got his son through college and law school.

CASE 5

1. At the age of sixteen, Edward A. said proudly that a phrenologist had examined his head and said that he would make a good lawyer. So he decided to study law.
2. The Wilsons have no worries about their son—an astrologer said that children born in May are great savers.

Problem II

What is being done today to help the individual make better adjustments to his environment?

CASE 1

In a certain industrial training school, in mechanical work, 100 young men were chosen by an experienced interviewer to enter training. They had good instruction and careful supervision; 60 succeeded in the work of the first year, 40 failed. The 40 were patiently reinstructed, prodded, tolerated for months, and finally dropped. . . . As a preliminary to an investigation of test possibilities, the young men had all been tested when they entered the course, and the scores put away for subsequent study. . . . Of those who had fallen below a certain score in the test, three-quarters had failed in the course. Of those who scored above this critical point, less than one-fifth had failed. . . . The next 100 apprentices were chosen by the same interviewer, but from those candidates only those who scored above the critical point were selected. Of these, only 17 failed and 83 were successful—a marked improvement.

CASE 2

The essential nature of the anecdotal method of personal analysis consists of at least four important procedures which must be carefully distinguished.

1. *Observing conduct:* the first of these procedures is the persistent and continuing observation of the conduct of the pupil, in and out of the classroom, by all the teachers and school officers who regularly or occasionally come into contact with him.

2. *Recording observations:* the second procedure is that of making a record of each significant observation in terms that are as concrete and objective as possible, and the filing of these records in some convenient manner so that they may be systematically assembled and studied in the central office.

3. *Periodical analysis and interpretation of anecdotes.*

4. *Remedial treatment:* if teachers know only that Pupil A is "rated" very low in honesty and truthfulness, there is usually very little that can be done about it; but if they know that his lies are confined to inventing imaginative excuses for tardiness, and his dishonesty to "losing" library books, there is neither cause of very serious concern nor lack of promising ways in which to approach the pupil with a view to developing better habits.

CASE 3

The personal history questionnaire, usually serving as a background for the interview, is one of the most common devices used in counseling. These questionnaires tend to become more and more elaborate, calling for as much information about the life history of the individual as it is possible to accumulate. When supplemented by the anecdotal or behavior record of the individual in school or in his employment, these studies make it possible to trace over long periods of time the tendencies, the characteristics, and the possibilities of the individual. The competent counselor, with this background, should be able to make constructive suggestion to the individual regarding present and future means of improvement.

CASE 4

Occupational analyses are growing more and more numerous and complete. By means of these detailed job feature outlines the individual has an opportunity to question every phase of any occupation he may be considering. Outlines for occupational analyses cover the following points: nature of work, main advantages and disadvantages, qualifications and training needed, possibilities and requirements, remuneration, hours of work, seasonal demands, organization of workers, entrance age, time required to learn duties, supply of labor, sources of labor supply, increasing or decreasing demands for labor, and common deficiencies of workers. The Rochester Institute of Technology, in a series of occupational analyses, including retailing, photography, chemistry, food administration, electrical and mechanical fields, etc., is attempting to set forth all the conditions in these fields of activity. The difficulties as well as the advantages are given so that no student need make the mistake of picturing an easy road to success in any of these fields.

Problem III

1. What progress is being made in industry and business in matching of individuals and occupations?

2. How do both management and the individual gain by better placement of employees?

CASE 1

One of the large manufacturing establishments, according to an old report, has as monarch of the hiring-on window a man who had the misfortune to lose one of his legs in the company's employ. As a result of this loss he was given his present life job, which he does to the queen's taste. He was induced to describe his methods, something like the following: "On Mondays I turn down all men with white collars, on Tuesdays all with blue eyes. Wednesdays all with dark eyes. Redheaded men I never hires, and there be days when I has a grouch on and hires every tenth man." [5]

[5] Link, H. C., *Employment Psychology*. New York: The Macmillan Co.

In many small industries the foreman or other production supervisor hires new employees from the line of applicants for work at the plant or from among his acquaintances. However, as size of establishment and number of distinct and specialized jobs make it more difficult for foremen to know the applicants personally, employment managers are engaged to specialize in the work of matching applicants and jobs. Many progressive industrial and business establishments now have "well-organized personnel departments, making use of application blanks, interviews, letters of recommendation, and perhaps even psychological and trade tests in the selection of workers."

CASE 2

The application blank is made out with a view to getting on record any information that may be needed in selection, placement, transfer, layoffs, training, or studies that may be undertaken in the interests of the plant as a whole. For example, in studying employees of the Yellow Cab Company of Philadelphia, Viteles found that the "good earner" among the cab drivers is an older man, married, with a number of dependents, physically fit, and who, on the whole, has stuck to such jobs as he has had for a number of years.[6] New and increasing government requirements for information regarding personnel are increasing the value of these detailed records.

CASE 3

One of the most widely used traditional methods in hiring and placing workers is the personal interview. As in the case of the application blank, the interview, regardless of its value in determining fitness for work, is a necessary feature of the hiring program and in transferring and promoting workers within the plant. In the case of the applicant the interview serves as a sort of introduction to the firm. It gives him an opportunity to obtain firsthand information concerning the character, policies, and plans of the company. At the same time the employment interviewer is placed in a position to make judgments on the appearance of the applicant as well as to engage in a general discussion of his interests, attitudes, and so on. The interview also gives an opportunity to arrive at fairly accurate estimates of temperamental and allied characteristics.[7]

[6] Viteles, M. S., *Op. cit.*
[7] *Ibid.*

Case 4

Elements in the modern induction process are suggested in these points taken from reported plans of a large western New York concern:

The foreman spends ample time with the new employee, outlining his duties, his chances for upgrading, and the general production scheme. He shows him lockers and lavatories and impresses safety regulations upon him. The foreman tells him his wage rate and makes clear the system of increases. Before turning the newcomer over to his assistant for job training, the foreman explains essentials of company plans and policies for workers' well-being— namely, paid vacations, illness and maternity benefits, life insurance provided by the company, accident and health insurance carried jointly by the worker and management, and arrangements for fixed payroll deductions. All such programs supplement Social Security provisions, and the foreman must be equally familiar with government and company measures so that he may be able to answer in detail any questions concerning either. He must also be quite as thoroughly at home with applications of other legislation relating to labor.

Case 5

According to an account in *Nation's Business*, the four Kaiser shipyards on San Francisco Bay hired 17,136 men and 10,059 quit during the month before *exit interviewers* went to work. These interviewers were able to cut the quitting lists in half. By helping these discontented workers to think through their problems, see points they had overlooked, and by transferring workers or by reporting for corrections many unsatisfactory conditions, the desire to look elsewhere for employment was materially lessened. The fuller understanding of individuals and conditions in the plants that come to personnel men, supervisors, and management from these interviewers suggest other values of this practice.

UNIT XII

Employee Training

Objectives

1. *To observe the interest held by industry and business in the continued training of employees after they have been hired.*
2. *To review training methods in current use.*
3. *To observe the increasing stress placed upon the training responsibilities of the line supervisors and to become a better trainer of workers.*
4. *To consider the reasons for increasing emphasis upon the training of supervisors and to take a more interested and aggressive attitude in one's own training problems.*

INTRODUCTION

As a preparation for the problems in this unit, groups should restudy carefully the first five headings in Unit III. Other principles of habit formation also apply to the very practical and universal problem of training on the job.

Where does most employee training take place? The answer to this question is so generally "on the job" that this phrase might well be used as the title for this unit. H. Moore reports studies indicating that much more than 75 per cent of all employee training is done on the job. While it is obvious that industry relies upon vocational schools, some types of apprentice-class setups, and the colleges for certain phases of training, it is equally obvious that such training must be rounded out or completed on the job. Leffingwell writes of training on the job: "It is without question the most effective plan to do the training; the worker deals with realities, realizes he is taking part in the actual work of the company, sees other workers doing the same kind of tasks and is spurred on to equal them, and forms habits easily and directly because he sees their necessity and value." [1]

Who is responsible for training? Training duties rest on each person in the organization who is responsible for the work of others. Each executive or supervisor should be responsible for the training of those whom he supervises, and for making sure that they in turn provide adequate training for those for whose activities they are responsible.

The basic principles of learning work-skills and their applications to job training have been known and discussed since World War I. Unusual training demands upon industry during World War II have resulted in two new developments:

1. In the appointment of training directors or co-ordinators in large numbers of industries, a step has been taken toward better planned programs with responsibilities more definitely fixed. This training director or co-ordinator is usually given a staff in proportion to the size of the organization of which he is a part. The relationships between these staff men and the personnel or industrial relations department are not entirely uniform, but the setting up of training as a specific function has given training definite recognition from top management, emphasized the training director's authority and responsibility, and tended to eliminate duplications of efforts and plans. The trainer is a *staff man* who works with and for the *line* organization, continuing the policy of making actual training activities a line function and rendering a service to the line foreman.

2. A second development has been the practical work done by the War Manpower Commission on the older five steps in training the worker on the job. The nation-wide program, known as Job Instructor Training, unquestionably has left an imprint on industrial training methods and has developed an interest that will be permanently influential. Samples of the development of the five-step outline and of the Job Breakdown Sheet are given in Problem I immediately following.

[1] Leffingwell, W. H., *Training Clerical Workers on the Job.* New York: McGraw-Hill Book Company, Inc.

Problem I

Each member of the study group should teach another member to do a job as he would train an employee in his plant. Each should fill out and retain from jobs done in the group the two job breakdown sheets provided in Problem II.

CASE 1

The following elaboration of the five steps in job training was developed in a group at the Rochester Institute of Technology during the early months of the Job Instructor Training Program:

Step 1. Prepare the learner. Make learner feel at home. . . . Introduce him to fellow employees. . . . Acquaint him with facilities. . . . Find out his previous experience related to the job at hand. . . . Be clear, calm, and friendly.

Steps 2 and 3. Explanation and demonstration. Explain what the job is. . . . Its relation to the finished product. . . . Quality standards. . . . Essential safety precautions. . . . Use same qualities of voice and manner as before

In presenting the job to the learner, *position* him so that he will see the performance as he would if he were doing it. . . . Present no more than the learner can grasp. . . . Have tools, materials, and equipment in order. . . . Do each operation just as you want it done. . . . Give clear, concise explanations as you go along. . . . Look out for "shop" terms that may not be clear. . . . Emphasize key points.

Repeat demonstration. . . . Ask questions frequently regarding next steps. . . . Ask for key points with reasons. . . . Have learner tell instructor how to do the job.

Step 4. Trial performance by learner. Check arrangement of tools and equipment. . . . Encourage learner to take his time. . . . Ask questions (*How? What? When? Where? Why?*) and otherwise encourage learner to explain essential steps and key points. . . . Recognize progress. . . . Clear up final difficulties. . . . Put learner on his own for a time. . . . Before leaving him, tell him whom to consult in case of difficulty.

Step 5. Job-habit fixation. Come back to learner to recheck performance. . . . Encourage questions. . . . Ask again regarding key points. . . . Emphasize that speed is secondary to correct habit formation at this early stage of his learning. . . . Let learner's needs determine frequency of follow-up calls. . . . Give full and frank information to him regarding his progress. . . . Judge when he is qualified to work under normal supervision.

CASE 2

A COMPLETED BREAKDOWN SHEET
FOR A LIGHT ASSEMBLY JOB

Part: *Thermometer*   Operation: *Front assembly*

Important steps in the operation	"Key points" (knacks, hazards, "feel," timing, special information)
1. Take thermometer off line.	
2. Place in "standards" and inspect.	Check scale for filling; check condition of screws; check "points" on tube against scale reading (rejects in proper trays).
3. Place glass on springs.	Test for placement by pressing down with fingers.
4. Place bezel on glass; insert sides at top and pull top into place.	Make certain that double lug is to the top.
5. Bow bezel with left hand; insert sides at bottom and pull bottom into place.	
6. Push glass down; force sides of bezel into position with tool.	
7. Inspect front assembly.	Make sure that bezel lies flat on glass.
8. Place thermometer on line.	

CASE 3

A COMPLETED BREAKDOWN SHEET
FOR A TYPICAL MACHINE JOB*

Part: *Magnet Shaft*   Operation: *In-feed grind on centerless grind*

Important steps in the operation	"Key points" (knacks, hazards, "feel," timing, special information)
1. Place piece on plate against regulating wheel.	"Knack"—don't catch on wheel.
2. Lower lever—feed.	Hold at end of stroke (count 1-2-3-4). Slow feed—where might taper. Watch—no oval grinding.
3. Raise lever—release.	
4. Gauge pieces periodically.	More often as approach tolerance.
5. Readjust regulating wheel as required.	Watch—no back lash.
6. Repeat above until finished.	
7. Check.	

* A lead man in a machine shop did this breakdown in five minutes. He uses this breakdown "as is" for men who have had some previous experience on centerless grinders. For inexperienced men he breaks up this operation into several "instruction units," striking off a detailed breakdown for each unit.

CASE 4

JOB BREAKDOWN SHEET
FOR TRAINING MAN ON NEW JOB*

Part: _____   Operation: _____

Important steps in the operation	"Key points" (knacks, hazards, "feel," timing, special information)

* To be filled out for a selected project.

Problem II

Follow a learner through the significant steps in a learning process and apply the basic laws of learning at each step.

CASE 1

	How much does he know about the job?	How much should you show him or tell him?
1. Employee starts on a *new* job:		
2. Employee arrives at a "plateau":		
3. Employee reaches standard rate for the job:		
4. Employee earns normal premium:		

	How long should you leave him without guidance?	Need you apply the Law of Effect? How apply it?
1. Employee starts on a *new* job:		
2. Employee arrives at a "plateau":		
3. Employee reaches standard rate for the job:		
4. Employee earns normal premium:		

Some notes on the significance of learning:

1. It is safe to say that all normal persons are born with urges to satisfy (*readiness*).

2. Each individual has to learn, for himself, how to satisfy these urges (*effect*).

3. We learn to do by doing (*use*). For example: we learn colors by seeing; sounds by hearing; tastes by tasting; pressures and weights by handling; odors by smelling.

4. Learning is aided by associating the unknown with the known; the learner must have some experience before he has anything "to tie instructions to."

Problem III

What are some other principles and practices in training, retraining, or upgrading employees?

CASE 1

"We must," writes a Rochester executive, "continually emphasize to all of our supervisors that Personnel is just as much a part of their job as getting work done. If we are to build an effective employee group we must get closer to the employee. It is a definite responsibility to have a common understanding with each man of what the company expects and how he measures up. To understand a man we must know something of his background, his social attitude, and his interests. *Each supervisor must appreciate that the measure of his success is the progress he has made in the development of those employees in his charge.* Without men, materials and machines mean nothing."

CASE 2

Firemen controlling the boilers and automatic stokers of a certain great power plant were thoroughly dissatisfied with their work, and the management was disturbed by the excessive cost of coal consumption. The men needed better training. To prepare a manual of instructions a fresh job analysis was undertaken. As an experiment, in one unit each separate boiler was equipped with additional gauges which for the first time showed each man just how efficiently he was managing his own boiler. Instantly a new spirit spread among the men. Rivalry sprang up. They began to ask the reasons for doing this and that. When the training manuals were ready, the workers already had an appetite for the new information. The experiment was extended throughout the works. The firemen were given a new status and called stoker operators. There was no more grumbling, no more talk of a strike.

CASE 3

The Goodyear Tire and Rubber Company formerly had a system under which labor-training foremen responsible to production general foremen were used for training workers. A tendency to neglect training in favor of production output led to the establishment of a separate Labor Training Division charged with responsibility for improving and devising training methods and carrying them into effect. There are four specific functions: training new labor; re-training old labor, when turned over by production departments; placing temporary surplus; and relocating misfits.

CASE 4

It has been estimated that about 15 per cent of the training necessary to produce an effective retail store staff can be given by the training staff, and that the remaining 85 per cent must be given in the departments. The buyers have this training done either by their assistants or by regular sales people designated as "sponsors," whose duties are to handle cases of training and retraining needs as they arise.

CASE 5

We had a rule when I was with a steamship company that no man in the shore forces was ready for promotion until he could as-sure management that his promotion would not, even temporarily, weaken the force. If the walking-boss aspired to the chief-steve-dore's job he had a hatch tender in training ready to take his own place and a stevedore trained and ready to drive the winch. The rule proved valuable in several respects. It committed management to a policy of promotion from within the ranks and it encouraged men in the lower grades. The winch driver studying the hatch ten-der's job was a better winch driver.[2]

CASE 6

A study made several years ago indicated that most foreman train-ing emphasized the progress, equipment, and material aspects of foremanship at the expense of the personnel aspects. Today, man-agement must develop better ways of training the supervisory staff in interpreting to the employees the personnel policies, plans, and procedures of the company and in translating to the top executives the misunderstandings, complaints, grievances, and irritations of employees. This two-way channel of information must be developed more effectively than it has been in the past. The foreman and other members of the supervisory forces must also be aided in developing better personal leadership skills and better ability for training-on-the-job. The efficient foreman of today must not only get production, but get this production *under modern employee relations*.

[2] Lindsey, L. J., *The Foreman and Industrial Executive.*

CASE 7

That the supervisor is the key to the training problem is suggested by Appley when he writes, "Ability to understand what other people are talking about, then to turn around and present it to someone else so he can understand it and to get him actually to put it into operation is not a common ability. And yet it is the one ability that should be developed on the part of supervisors and executives." [3]

CASE 8

An illustration of the importance of having employees in a continuing training program may well be shown by this experience of one large company:

The management had found it expedient to change from coal to gas in its power plants. Much of the employees' work had been entirely manual under coal operation. Using gas as a fuel necessitated retraining these men in a mental type of work—observing gauges, recording data, and making adjustments to the semiautomatic central apparatus. This retraining probably could not have been carried out in a business less alert to training responsibilities.

[3] Appley, L. A., *Personnel.*

UNIT XIII

Personnel

Objectives

1. *To review the development of modern human relations practices over a series of years.*
2. *To develop attitudes of open-minded inquiry.*
3. *To contribute to the willingness of all parties concerned to give and take in the settlement of issues affecting the welfare of all.*

INTRODUCTION

About 6,000 years ago, in what is believed to be the oldest complete book in the world, an ancient Egyptian said:

"If you are in the position of one to whom petitions are made, be courteous and listen to the petitioner's story. Do not stop his words until he has poured out all that is in his heart and has said all that he came to say. A man with a grievance loves the official who will accept what he states and let him talk out his troubles fully. A kind word will illuminate his heart, but if an official stops the flow of his words people will say, 'Why should that fellow have the power to behave in this way?'"

This entire course has been devoted to key problems in personnel relations. This unit is designed as a review of all that has gone before. The aim of this introductory reading is to present a review of the thinking of leaders in personnel administration over the past three or four decades. For this purpose, several dated statements, each representing the personnel point of view at the time it was made, are included. The student may find it interesting to compare the statement of any one period with that of any other.

153

BACKGROUNDS

Three distinct stages in the development of modern personnel practices are termed by Channing R. Dooley: the *period of
dictation*, the *period of paternalism*, and the *period of co-
operation*.

"I do not know when the pendulum began to swing away
from the period of dictation, possibly in the 1890's or early
1900's. About that time, when I was working in the shops, I
remember coming home one evening and hearing an associate
who worked in the local steel mills say, 'The boss fired a man
today for wearing a red necktie.' I think it would be safe to say
that most of our big industries were founded and developed
under a leadership of dictation, usually by some outstanding
man of great ability. Frontiers had to be conquered, and great
obstacles had to be overcome. This method was the order of the
day—typical of the times.

"By and by times became easier. A majority of the industrial
leaders had made a great deal of money. They had time to
look around and consider the welfare of their employees, and
they genuinely wanted to do something for the betterment of
conditions. Mr. Carnegie gave libraries to hundreds of com-
munities. Mr. Pullman built for his employees houses equipped
with modern plumbing, but the story goes that bathtubs were
used for coal bins. Mr. Paterson beautified the streets and
homes of Dayton at his own expense and of his own motives. In
a brief time the pendulum swung from extreme dictation to
extreme paternalism, which, by the way, was just as displeas-
ing to employees as the old order of autocracy.

"Then the war (First World War) came, and we got busy
with a great many other things. When the war was over, things
began to take a different shape. If an employee had the tooth-
ache, we did not send him home, but we put a dentist in the
factory, not simply because we felt sorry for the man, but because we wanted him on the job. Management and men sat
around council table to discuss their problems, not because

one side was sorry for the other, but because intelligence rather than emotion had introduced a new phase of employer-employee relationship—the stage of *co-operation*. And this co-operative idea will continue just as long as company interest and company loyalty plus pooled intelligence continue to make for increased efficiency."

THREE TRENDS MERGE (1931)

In 1931, Edward S. Cowdrick said, "Personnel administration, in the present-day sense of the term, was the outgrowth of three distinct activities in industry: Employment, education and training programs, and the varied services formerly grouped under the term 'welfare work.' Labor needs of the war period found the employment manager, the educational supervisor, and the welfare director already established in many business institutions. They were promptly drafted into the new vocation of industrial relations management, where they were joined by recruits from all sources and equipped with all varieties of experience, qualifications, and background. . . . All sorts of methods for regulating the relationships between employers and employees were devised. It appeared that a new profession of labor management had sprung up, fully manned, almost overnight. In place of the modest employment man and the struggling social service worker there was the director of industrial relations.

"Industrial relations management grew and prospered. Personnel staffs in many companies were expanded to impressive proportions. Then came the business depression of 1920–22 and with it came the swift deflation of much that was unsubstantial in this development of personnel management. Confronted with stern financial necessity, many companies abolished their industrial relations departments. Others pruned them mercilessly and cut down their functions to the barest necessities. At this late date managing executives probably will admit that many of their number in those days were not wholly displeased at the departure of the uplifters and indulged the hope—sometimes secretly, sometimes openly expressed—that they would not return.

"Nor did they return—as 'uplifters.' Some did not come back at all, but went into other vocations. But a nucleus of labor administrators who had built up their work on sound principles and according to business methods stuck to their jobs or soon returned to them. Even at the bottom of the depression enlightened employers realized that good labor relations were vital to business success.

"By the time business activity again turned downward in 1929, labor management had established itself as an integral part of industry—a function that brought tangible benefits to workers and managers alike, and that could not be discarded without definite loss. This chain of events largely accounts for the survival of industrial relations programs and personnel departments in the depression of 1930.

"But alongside this coming of age of industrial relations management and this adjustment of its functions to those of the general administration of industry, there was another development of equal or greater significance. Reference already has been made to the *increased interest of managing executives in the human problems of their industries*. The importance of this development scarcely can be overestimated. Its extent is not realized even by the executives concerned. In constantly increasing measure the highest officials of corporations are taking personal responsibility for labor relationships. In more than one large company industrial relations policies originate with the president.

"The change has come about partly on account of the growing public interest in employer-employee relationships and the increasing disposition to hold management responsible for the adjustment and maintenance of these relationships on terms of fairness and harmony. Partly it has been due to a recognition of the enlarged importance of wage earners as the consumers of the products of industry. Largely, however, it has been a natural evolution, accelerated by the adoption of modern in-

dustrial relations practices and advanced methods of collective
dealing between management and employees. To the extent
that *managing executives have become personnel-minded,*
industrial relations management has achieved one of its most
important and most difficult tasks." [1]

EFFECTS OF DEPRESSION (1934)

The National Industrial Conference Board in studying "The
Effects of the Depression on Industrial Relations Programs"
(1934) classified these activities in six broad groups: (a) Financial benefit activities, (b) Medical and social activities,
(c) Education and training activities, (d) Employer-employee
dealings, (e) Employment procedure, (f) Personnel records
and staff. The concluding summary of this report is as follows:

"The continued prevalence of industrial relations activities
during the depression, indicated by the data presented in this
study, shows that such activities have become regular and
necessary features of company policy. Otherwise they could
not have survived a period of drastic financial retrenchment.

"That industrial relations policies have an even more important function to perform under conditions brought about by
the National Industrial Recovery Act is the opinion of many
industrial executives. The question of wages and hours was the
principal problem of personnel management, according to the
replies of 66 companies. Reduction of working hours and work
spreading made it difficult or impossible to provide sufficient
work to assure regular employees what they considered an
adequate income, with the result that discontent was aroused.
Combined with the work spreading under code requirements
was the difficulty in securing adequate business to permit
operation for the maximum workweek allowed. Between code
restrictions, on one side, and poor business on the other, plant
executives found themselves in a difficult position.

"Executives are not in agreement with regard to the general
effect of the Recovery Act on industrial relations. Of those who

[1] *Personnel Series, No. 11.* American Management Association.

158 PERSONNEL

expressed their views, 26 believed that employer-employee relations had improved, but 51, nearly twice as many, held the opposite view. Causes for improvement in relations that were cited included increased wages and reduced hours, more stable employment, closer contact and understanding between management and working force, employee representation plans, quick settlement of disputes, and a better understanding on the part of both employer and employee of each other's problems.

"Changes in wages and working hours were also given as reasons for more unsatisfactory employer-employee relations. Shortened hours brought unwelcome reductions in earnings, and work spreading caused hardship to the older and long-service employees. Propaganda in newspapers and on the radio and statements by persons prominent in the national administration were cited as contributing to a general condition of labor unrest."

Particular personnel plans and policies will no doubt continue to vary from year to year, but in the last analysis the success or failure of any personnel procedure will depend upon the attitude or spirit in which it is carried out by first-line supervisors in charge. Even a cash bonus may be handed to a man in such a way as to arouse his resentment. On the other hand, a right attitude toward individuals may sustain morale in the face of very discouraging financial conditions.

GOVERNMENT INFLUENCE (1937)

After reviewing two previous stages in the history of industrial relations, (a) "The so-called welfare activities stage" and (b) "The stage which was marked by the introduction of personnel management as a staff function to promote more directly and adequately employer-employee relations in industry," Clarence G. Stoll, Western Electric Company, says:

"We are apparently entering a third stage marked by government legislation, directed, in part at least, toward shaping industrial relations for us. The best preventive of government intrusion in this field is for industry to make more rapid strides in the development of constructive employer-employee relations."

PERSONNEL WINS STANDING (1940)

"To understand what has occurred in the relations of management and workers in recent years," writes J. Walter Dietz, "one must deliberately set out to look for the tidal changes. . . . I believe the change that is of greatest importance lies in the fact that personnel policies have found their place amid the consequential matters upon which the best executive thinking is done and are part and parcel of the essential problems that must be considered in running a business enterprise. In short, personnel policies have moved into the front office of business. . . . The trend is definitely toward a clear, clean-cut statement of management's intended standard of treatment in all human relationships within a business. More companies have stated their personnel policies in the last two years than ever before."

GOVERNMENTAL INFLUENCE GROWING (1944)

This titular statement represents a consensus of a number of personnel men rather than the point of view of any one individual.

The outstanding feature of recent months has been the unprecedented growth of government controls. These include procurement of manpower for the armed forces, relative freezing of wage rates, manpower stabilization under controlled recruiting, negotiated and canceled contracts, controlled inventories, and priorities.

The production section of our economic life, under pressure for a type of finished product practically new to it in the era of nonmilitary expectations, has made astounding progress in the face of scheduling and planning difficulties imposed by the sudden replacement of experienced with inexperienced employees. Problems of scheduling and planning have been complicated by priorities, uncertainty, interrupted supply, and inflated costs. These costs, often due to overtime operations and competitive purchasing in spite of price ceilings, have introduced new variables for accounting and records departments. Depleted in force and materials, the maintenance group has kept the gear of the plunging fullback in sufficiently good shape so that ground has been consistently gained against heartbreaking odds.

In the midst of all this feverish activity, observers note the development of closer social or group feeling among the men behind the men behind the guns. Intolerance has of necessity diminished. Taxation has increased to such a point that the rich and the poor are closer together in purchasing power. War savings have given many a financial backlog for the first time. That there has been a lowering of the general standard of living is questioned by very few. However, opinions differ on whether prewar standards will return during the lifetime of the present generation. Many feel that individual initiative is being stifled and that a premium is being placed on improvidence rather than upon frugality and foresight. Yet, the fact still remains that few take exception to the "American Way" or point to any better place than America in which to live.

All of these forces and influences have worked together to raise to a new high the recognition of the personnel function. There has been much more extensive application of personnel principles and policies. More top executives have become personnel minded, and competent personnel managers are now an integral part of their companies' councils.

Some of the functions of personnel and industrial relations which have currently expanded or developed are color engineering, employee counseling, new employee induction, handbooks, employee suggestion systems, personal services for individual employees, use of placement tests, establishment of cafeterias, music during working hours, noon-hour recreation facilities, clinical approach to problems, and employee magazines and papers.

In the immediate and the postwar future many adjustments will have to be made that are now unpredictable. How can re-absorption of service men and women be accomplished without summary dismissal or other harsh treatment of good workers trained under the war emergency? What other problems will industry face in returning from war to peacetime production? What will be the taxation demands of the future? What will be the size and influence of the Army and Navy of the future?

Whatever the problems now emerging or definitely foreseen, there are a few fundamentals that all supervisors would do well to review and learn to recognize. Employee attitudes reflect good or poor supervision and good or poor policies. Good policies are of little effect if they are not well administered. Any developments from which a company is to profit must benefit the individual employees, and these employees must see this result. We have all read of the basic interrelationships of the three "M's"—Men, Money, and Machines. The "M" for men must be in every combination, or the others do not function. Attention is being focused as never before upon the individual. His best efforts come through the recognition and the satisfaction of his human desires and ambitions. Recent surveys agree that these desires or ambitions are, in order, security, opportunity for advancement, and recognition as a worthwhile individual in an essential activity.[2]

CO-OPERATION AND CONFERENCE (1948)

The spokesman for the same personnel group who prepared the above statement for 1944 has added the following appraisal of the situation as of 1948:

"In recent years there has been a substantial growth of Government controls related to a number of items which affect our daily relationships and activities. These continue to be a factor which must be regarded in our thinking.

"For instance, the statement has been made that there are three interests in conducting a business—Management, Labor,

[2] Roper, Elmo, *American Mercury* and *Management Review*.

and Government. In any event, it is apparent that progress is to be made only through co-operation and conferences as opposed to conflict. Such a statement brings us back to the cycle of activities within a business and should stress the fact that none of them can be neglected if the business is to survive. These activities, simply stated, include engineering, planning, supervision, production, sales, accounting, and merchandising. They are necessary to attract the investment of capital which, in turn, provides for the purchase of machinery, the salaries essential to securing and retaining personnel, who in turn develop processes and methods.

"The fact still remains that unless an attractive product can be offered for sale to an interested consumer at a reasonable price and with a reasonable margin of profit there will be no industry. This is apt to be even more true in the future with the necessity for taxes related to problems and projects such as those involved in world feedings, Veterans Administration functions, Social Security, labor-management developments and the legislative effect of current economic forces. Co-operation is not a one-way route but means an intelligent appraisal and a willingness to give and take in connection with problems and considerations which affect the welfare of all."

Problem I

Do you consider it a fair statement that good personnel or employer-employee relations depend primarily upon attitudes of all parties concerned?

CASE 1

From a variety of surveys of employee attitudes conducted almost continuously from 1933 to 1944 Elmo Roper reports the following four outstanding desires of American workmen:

1. *Security.* Three times as many workmen believe that guaranteed annual wages are important as believe the same thing about a voice for labor in management. Steady employment is a paramount consideration to ten times as many workers as is high pay, and to twenty-five times as many as are short hours.

2. *Advancement.* The second desire of labor is the chance to advance—just the good old American opportunity to get on in the world. Twice as many factory workers rate as important an opportunity for promotion as those so rating safeguarding seniority rights.

3. *Being treated like human beings.* This comes out in expressions of desires for clean surroundings, foremen who don't swear at their men, or a friendliness in the plant that preserves the identity of Jim or Charley instead of turning him into number 3098 on a cold-blooded payroll.

4. *Simple human dignity or recognition.* Most workers want to feel that they are personally performing creditably in a job which contributes something to the aggregate of human security, advancement, or happiness.

Are these attitudes common to supervisors as well as to workers?

How may taking them into consideration influence the treatment of subordinates by those in authority over them?

Can a supervisor give an employee a substantial sense of satisfaction in any one of these four basic desires without affording some satisfaction in the others?

Case 2

Joe was told to do a certain job and to have it done by a certain time, or else . . .

What supervisory principles can you think of that would apply to this case?

Could problems have arisen that might have been prevented?

What would you have wanted or needed to know before assigning the job to the employee?

What about this supervisor's attitude toward Joe?

Case 3

The first thing Supervisor X tells a new employee in his department is, "You are working *with* not *for* this company."

To what extent can it be said that the attitude of management is reflected by that of supervisors?

Do employees, in turn, reflect the attitude of their supervisors?

What do you find to be the attitude of old-timers? Are they proud of their associations, or are they sour and belittling?

Problem II

*The principles involved in the following cases have been called
"The Big Four" in good supervision. Identify these principles
and modify the list if you think it should be changed.*

Case 1

"In a survey conducted by a national organization among a large
group of mercantile employees, the preponderance of employee replies stated that recognition was the most important consideration,
while their employers judged that it was wages. To me this is not
surprising, because I have heard supervisory people state that if
there were anything wrong with a man's work he would be told of
it and that any man who did not receive a 'bawling out' should
realize that his work was satisfactory. Not long ago I was talking
with one of our men who had been mentioned as good supervisory
timber. I asked him how he was getting along, and here was his
reply: 'I don't know, Mr. Bruce. In the fifteen years I have worked
here no one has ever criticized or commended me on the job I
have done. I really don't know where I stand.'" [3]

Would this be satisfactory to you? Why?

Do people respond to approval? What inference do you draw
from the term "bawling out?"

Is the candidate ready for a supervisory job? Do you think he
will do a good job with those under him?

What fundamental stimulus of human behavior has been neglected?

Case 2

"If ten people witness an automobile accident, there usually are
ten versions of what happened, because of marked variance of
interest and points of view. By the same token you can find as much
variation among supervisory people of what we should consider the
qualifications of a good employee. A sound rating plan will correct
this problem. An effective rating plan must be objective. I prefer
to call them *progress reports*. At any stage in a man's development,
his progress report should show his standing at the time with reference to the full requirements of the job." [4]

Do you agree? Why?

[3] Bruce, R. M., *Address*. General Session, U. S. Independent Telephone Association.

[4] *Ibid.*

Is it possible for a talented man merely to be coasting and yet show up better on a rating sheet than an unskilled man who is giving the job his best efforts? Which would you prefer?

CASE 3

"There is a lot more to the reduction of accidents than just talking safety. An employee who is worrying about his finances or difficulties at home isn't thinking about the last message on the safety bulletin. If he is not up to par physically, he may offer a real hazard. If he is worrying about his progress he is not thinking safety. In other words, our entire employee relations program may have its effects on our accident record. I have been surprised at how little encouragement is needed to bring about a consciousness of keeping physically fit. Annual medical examinations give the doctor an opportunity to counsel with employees—to show them how easy it is to correct a condition if treatment is started early." [5]

Can "safety consciousness" be made a habit?

How does this square with previously discussed definitions of attitudes?

Compare the effectiveness of this attitude with that of good, mechanical safety devices. If you had to get along with either one alone, which would you prefer?

CASE 4

1. "It is possible that in standardizing the framework around which so much of the discussions in the present-day foremanship training conference revolves, training specialists have over-emphasized mechanical methods of handling typical supervisory problems and have thereby failed to develop that desirable attitude of the supervisor toward the job that carries over into his daily contacts with subordinates. If this should prove to be the case, it would account for the fact that, despite the great effort being made to improve supervision (and thereby employee morale), we continue to observe poor morale, little or no reduction in the frequency and severity of accidents, and unheard-of increases in absenteeism and turnover. Less emphasis on the search for methods, and increased accent on a proper spirit toward the supervisor's job, almost certainly will improve our present foremanship training programs." [6]

[5] *Ibid.*

[6] Cooper, G. M., *Personnel.* American Management Association.

2. A leading, current text in industrial psychology asserts that in an army, a school system, or an industrial plant, there is no substitute for morale; and that morale can neither be legislated, induced by logical argument, nor bought for a price. After paying due tribute to the outworn expression, "hiring hands," the author says:

"The whole man is always hired, and the whole man brings to work a good many things besides his hands. He brings the effects of too many or too few spankings as a child; of whether he won or lost in last night's card game; of whether his wife sent him to work with a scolding or a kiss; of whether or not the company 'docked' his wages when he was home last week with a sick child. Such things are of vital importance in determining an employee's real value to a company. And, such things as these, considered together for the whole working force, determine the morale of an industrial plant." [7]

What is meant by "personnel mindedness"?

To what extent do you feel that these two case statements serve as a summary of the course you are now completing?

[7] Tiffin, Joseph, *Industrial Psychology*. New York: Prentice-Hall, Inc.

UNIT XIV

Analysis of Supervisory Activities

This outline of supervisory activities, or duties, has been studied, discussed, and otherwise checked against current practice by individuals, conference groups, and committees for more than twenty years.

Materials for the original draft of this comprehensive list of duties or activities of supervisors, or foremen, were collected from (a) group discussions in supervisory conferences, (b) management magazines, reports, and books, and (c) direct observations in Rochester industrial establishments. Copies of this first list were placed in the hands of approximately 100 foremen studying at the Rochester Institute of Technology. These men reviewed the lists, discussed them with various groups in their own plants, and turned them back with criticisms and additions. The list, as revised in the light of these contributions, was studied by the faculty of the institute, and other alterations were made. Finally, the analysis was studied by the Training Committee of the Rochester Industrial Management Council.

Within recent years, this committee of the Industrial Management Council submitted its most thoroughgoing set of additions and alterations. Prefatory to the present list, the committee writes:

"The following outline of Supervisory Activities is considered to be complete in that the items common to all levels of supervision regardless of sex or the operation supervised have been included. These items are present in some degree in any supervisory job. It is not exhaustive, as it would not be possible to list all minor variations of supervisors' functions wherever they might exist. No attempt has been made to evaluate the degree of decision or responsibility, and, of course, it must be understood that a supervisor's authority on any of these items can only be exercised within the limit of his assignment and within the prescribed policy established by his employer."

I. GENERAL RESPONSIBILITIES

Development of knowledge, personal traits, relationships, and impressions within and without the company and department:

A. To be familiar with steps and methods of all jobs supervised (helpful, but not essential, to be able to perform some of the jobs supervised).

B. To be "reasonable" as opposed to being "hardboiled," benevolent, or other extremes; co-operative with regular duties and matters of company interest:
   1. Develops feeling of responsibility for work success in employees.
   2. Gives praise and criticism objectively in terms of work results —not in personal terms of likes and dislikes.
   3. Is willing and able to explain method of payment, matters of policy and operation.
   4. Encourages suggestions and development of new procedures.
   5. Consults group for pertinent information before making decisions.

C. To know the sources and bounds of his own authority, and to act accordingly.

D. To understand channels of communication from top management through himself to those affected below.

E. To know his job in itself and in relation to other departments.

F. To give recognition to employees as individuals and analyze their social contacts and desires:
   1. Understands social structure of groups.
   2. Leads his group—encourages natural group leaders to act.
   3. Develops individual feeling of belonging within the group:
      a. Encourages participation.
      b. Stimulates group to function under its own internal drive.
      c. Encourages group to participate in planning and scheduling.
      d. Develops a spirit of co-operation.
   4. Is aware of attitudes, customs, and sentiments which affect production.

5. Knows the traits, ideas, and efficiency of each employee.
6. Gets things done without apparent "bossing."
7. Credits ideas and performance; recognizes ambitions.

G. To so conduct his work and department that unannounced inspections or visitors are not embarrassing.

H. To promote safety:
1. Maintains housekeeping.
2. Promotes individual precautions and care.

I. Without reluctance, to permit his employees to talk to his supervisor or the personnel department.

J. To strive to improve his own efficiency and training:
1. Pays attention to requirements of job.
2. Sets example by personal conduct:
   a. Is prompt in arrival and keeping promises.
   b. Is friendly, co-operative, loyal.
   c. Is neat in work and appearance.
   d. Obeys safety and other rules.
   e. Participates in community, civic, social affairs.
   f. Gives precise and clear instructions.
3. Confers with and promotes co-operation between other supervisors (up, down, laterally).
4. Attends group conferences and departmental meetings.
5. Studies technical subjects related to his job.
6. Keeps up-to-date on policy changes, stemming from legislation, particularly on compensation, labor relations, discrimination, organization, wages and hours, Social Security, unemployment insurance, etc.
7. Observes effect of his own conduct on others and his ability to handle people.
8. Seeks first in himself the cause of inefficiency or shortcomings.
9. Delegates as much detail as possible (including necessary authority).
10. Does not take things for granted; is active in "follow-up" (particularly checking results).

II. Planning

Anticipation and control of items which may adversely affect personnel or quality, quantity, and cost of product:

A. To establish long range objectives:
1. Sets up program to acquire maximum personal effectiveness (knowledge, conduct and creation of favorable impression).
2. Uses wide perspective in determining departmental needs:

     a. Decides type of personnel and training.
     b. Plans safety measures and practices.
     c. Exercises controls.
     d. Develops understudies and promotes flexibility.
     e. Trains and absorbs new employees.
     f. Procures and lays out equipment.

B. To anticipate current requirements of activities and problems far enough in advance to notify and enable others to do a good job:
1. Selects, places, and trains personnel.
2. Effectively applies employee effort (advance assignment of work).
3. Procures mechanical or material requirements:
     a. Establishes machine schedules.
     b. Establishes labor schedules.
     c. Arranges availability of tools, equipment, materials, supplies.
4. Assists in departmental layout and equipment selection.
5. Estimates and determines status of jobs in process.
6. Practices preventative maintenance through periodic inspections.
7. Develops accident prevention through periodic inspections and educating employees to think safely.
8. Uses budget and other reports for control purposes.
9. Outlines use of own time to allow latitude for follow-up and employee contacts.
10. Anticipates and corrects conditions causing grievances.
11. Keeps own supervisor informed, so he in turn can make effective use of knowledge.

III. Personnel

Conduct and attitude towards employees supervised, and ability to secure production of highest quality and quantity at minimum cost:

A. To constitute the key to effective personnel relations:
1. Recommends or approves assignments, requests for leave of absence, transfers, placement, suspension or dismissal and evaluation of employee merit.
2. Assists in the classification or evaluation of positions.
3. Deals with salary and wage matters within the limitations of policy, law or contract.
4. Selects and places new employees in co-operation with the

personnel department and his own supervisors (anticipating
needs to enable others to do a good job).

5. Assigns employees to jobs and directs their work.
6. Promptly clears up all real or imaginary grievances.
7. Recommends promotions.
8. Deals with employees or their representatives within authority and established policy.
9. Works closely with counselors and other employee relations
staff, recognizing their specialty.
10. Encourages employees to have confidence in him and con-
fide in him.
11. Is concerned with the safety and health of his employees on
a preventative as well as a corrective basis.
12. Controls and accounts for time worked.
13. Evaluates and follows up employees:
    a. Observes from day to day and hour to hour.
    b. Rates periodically and lets employees know how they
    stand.
    c. Rates objectively.
    d. Talks with individual employees about their ratings.
14. Instills a sense of responsibility in employees.
15. Is open-minded and co-operative in transfers and promotions.
16. Keeps own supervisor informed on attitudes, conditions and
any unusual items.

B. To teach and train:
1. Teaches on the job in connection with regular production activities.
2. Analyzes training needs.
3. Inducts and orients, trains and follows up new and transferred employees.
4. Sets up nonfinancial incentives as aids to learning.
5. Develops understudies and substitutes for each job, including his own.
6. Programs personal study to qualify for emergencies and
promotion.
7. Learns and follows tried and accepted methods of instruction.
8. Encourages outside study and courses.
9. Promotes flexibility of ability within work group.
10. Programs upgrading of employees and follows it.
11. Develops discipline through a desire to co-operate rather
than by invoking penalties.

C. To deal realistically in unpleasant, disputable, and emotional matters:
1. Recognizes defective work, low production, poor attitudes, absenteeism, etc.
2. Does not ignore such situations or take wrong steps in correcting them.
3. Analyzes such situations to determine the cause.
4. Is firm and decisive in disciplinary matters.
5. Holds corrective interviews with workers.
6. Reviews and adjusts grievances; discusses or explains reasons for not adjusting.
7. Carefully prepares dismissal cases (does not retain unsatisfactory operators unduly long).
8. Turns in a factual report on employees for transfer or termination.
9. Establishes a record of fairness free from partiality or discrimination.

IV. QUALITY OF WORK

Ability to influence employees to attain a high-grade product:
A. To pay attention to use of materials, equipment, effort, and to prevent waste.
B. To analyze tasks assigned and strive to have them performed expeditiously.
C. To present to his superior suggestions and recommendations which he cannot inaugurate alone.
D. To consult workers about suggestions and improvements.
E. To be responsible for meeting process specifications:
1. Meets and maintains established quality standards.
2. Follows up and secures approval of changes in procedure.
3. Makes experimental runs.
4. Questions material quality and reasons for defect.
5. Makes recommendations on changes.
F. To be responsible for inspection of parts:
1. Appeals differences of opinion.
2. Makes salvage decisions.
3. Approves work offered for inspection.
G. To be responsible for determining or changing operating procedures, unless of engineering or major status.

V. QUANTITY OF WORK

Ability to influence employees to produce at their most effective capacity (see also II, Planning, and III, Personnel):

A. To be responsible for meeting schedules (prearrange necessary details):
1. Orders necessary replacement and additional tools, jigs, fixtures, etc.
2. Determines machine schedules.
3. Determines labor schedules.
4. Requisitions supplies.
5. Follows up on material releases.
6. Authorizes machine set-up changes.
7. Follows up equipment layout changes.
8. Approves and secures necessary production records.
9. Authorizes casual overtime.
10. Stocks adequate small tools and materials for next shift.
11. Records status of incomplete work at end of shift.
12. Notifies following shift of continuing problems.
13. Replans work following a breakdown.
14. Makes shortages reports.
15. Devises procedures—including arrangement of work.
B. To maintain practical and simple controls as a follow-up.
C. To give attention to standards of performance and accomplishment:
1. Lets employee know what constitutes a good day's work.
2. Checks actual performance against standards.
D. To provide maintenance:
1. Authorizes and checks repairs.
2. Checks proper maintenance of production machines.
3. Checks use of standards, jigs, gauges and fixtures.
4. Reports breakdowns to proper authorities.

VI. Cost

Ability to produce quality and quantity at minimum cost:
A. To be cost conscious and make employees so:
1. Makes effective use of materials and equipment.
2. Prevents waste.
B. To conserve power, gas, light, water, compressed air, etc.
C. To conserve materials and supplies.
D. To strive for quality at minimum cost through inspection of work and tools.
E. To supply time and cost data to planning, accounting, and personnel departments.
F. To hold up questionable work until authoritatively passed upon.
G. To assign proper grades of labor to job.

H. To assign employees in accordance with ability.
 I. To train employees to meet quality and quantity standards.
 J. To improve and approve methods established by others.
 K. To take necessary action to meet budget.
 L. To suggest possible changes in product to effect economy.
 M. To approve indirect budgets.
 N. To grant permission to exceed budgets temporarily.
 O. To estimate standards for direct labor prior to setting of regular standards.

VII. SUMMARY

Participation in activities essential to producing quality products at acceptable costs in accordance with schedules, including planning and following up with due regard to safety, employee relations, and company policies.

Index

MI